Christianity certainly is a fact but the kind of fact that can only be believed.

Faith is the immediacy after reflection.

To believe the forgiveness of one's sins is the decisive crisis whereby a human being becomes spirit; he who does not believe this is not spirit.

Infinite humiliation and grace, and then a striving born of gratitude — this is Christianity.

The Holy Scriptures are the highway signs; Christ is the way.

Silence is the essence of the inner life.

"A genius may be a century ahead of his time, and therefore appear to be a paradox, but ultimately the race will assimilate what was once a paradox in such a way that it is no longer paradoxical."

Søren Kierkegaard
Of the Difference Between a Genius and an Apostle, 1847

TRUE GENIUS SERIES

A genius is a person who, in his or her field of expertise, discovers or creates something new that has the power to take humanity beyond previous ideas and concepts. The history of humanity can be seen as a series of creative "leaps" from past knowledge to new understanding Originally, the word genius meant to be possessed by a spirit. For a Christian, this means to be guided by the Spirit of the Creator in whose image he is made. This series is an introduction to some of the true geniuses throughout history who benefitted mankind and credited their achievements to their Creator.

Also Coming In this series:

Michelangelo: An Angel in the Stone
Beethoven and Beyond
Einstein: Discovering the Creator
Tolstoy: Rebel With a Story

SØREN KIERKEGAARD: AN AUTHENTIC LIFE
by Ben Alex
Copyright © 1997 Scandinavia Publishing House,
Nørregade 32, DK–1165 Copenhagen K., Denmark
Telephone: 45-33140091   Fax: 45-33320091

Text & Photo copyright © 1997 Ben Alex
Kierkegaard Reader: English text copyright © Princeton University Press
and © Augsburg Fortress Publishers
Idea, Photography and Graphic Design by Ben Alex
Cover Painting by Luplau Janssen, 1903 (The National Historical Museum, Frederiksborg, Denmark)
A co-production from Scandinavia Publishing House
Production: Grafikken, Denmark. Printed in Singapore

All rights reserved. No part of this book may be reproduced or utilized in any form or by any means, electronic or mechanical, including photocopying, recording, or by any information storage and retrieval system, without permission in writing from the Publisher.
ISBN 87 7247 495 5

I am grateful to Bishop Per Lønning in Norway, Professor Howard Hong in Minnesota, and General Secretary Niels-Jørgen Cappelørn of the Kierkegaard Research Center, Copenhagen, Denmark, for their suggestions and encouragement. Special thanks to Anne de Graaf, in The Netherlands, for her exceptional editing.

For Dave Kopp

SØREN KIERKEGAARD: AN AUTHENTIC LIFE

The Life and Writings of a Christian Philosopher

Text and Photos by
Ben Alex

Scandinavia

Contents

6 *PREFACE:* ENCOUNTER WITH SØREN KIERKEGAARD

10 CHRISTIANITY – A MESSAGE ABOUT EXISTENCE

12 *PART I:* FACES OF A RELIGIOUS GENIUS

LEYAH JENSEN

16 SON
TWELVE-YEAR-OLD MICHAEL CURSES GOD
A VISIT TO SÆDDING
Interview with Anders Stengaard

24 LOVER
WORKING ON LOVE
Interview with Pia Søltoft

LISTENING TO THE SILENCE
Kierkegaard and Nature
32

AUTHOR
THE MASTER AND THE SECRETARY
KIERKEGAARD AROUND THE WORLD
Interview with Kinya Masugata
THE LITERARY WORKS
36

PHILOSOPHER
A PHILOSOPHY OF HOPE
Interview with Howard Hong
44

WITNESS
MARTYR OF LAUGHTER
A PHILOSOPHY APPLIED *Interview with Per Lønning*
54

THE INNER LIFE
Kierkegaard and Prayer
66

PART II: A KIERKEGAARD READER
70

CHRONOLOGICAL SURVEY **118**
BIBLIOGRAPHY **120**

Encounter With Kierkegaard

A Personal Preface by Ben Alex

It was a cold and rainy December morning and I was back in Denmark. Downtown Copenhagen was bustling with bikes, cars and buses. Pedestrians rushed past me on their way to work and important appointments. The street of Vesterbrogade felt like a river of noise and confusion, all threatening to knock me down and sweep me away.

I stood on a street corner, holding onto my umbrella as tears ran down my cheeks, tears of both sadness and joy. It felt so good to be home, back home in the city where I had grown up. I had left Copenhagen eleven years earlier for a lonely existence in the high desert of Oregon. I had suffered much in that desert, not least from the consequences and remorse of past mistakes and choices that had finally caught up with me, and the loss of people I loved. After eleven years, when I was feeling the most hurt and confused, I had decided to go home. I was hoping to make restitution for my past and get back in touch with the God of my youth. Now, as I stood on that noisy street not knowing where to turn and with no immediate hope of a rendezvous, I felt more confused and lonely than ever. I looked up and spotted a gray building I had visited with my father when I was a child. It was the city museum, a forbidding building set behind a black iron fence. I walked through the gate and browsed through the exhibition.

On the second floor, in a modest room which other visitors seemed to have overlooked, I found some furniture and other items that had once belonged to Søren Kierkegaard.

> *I stood on a street corner, holding onto my umbrella as tears ran down my cheeks, tears of both sadness and joy.*

Like most other Danes, I did not know much about my famous fellow countryman, except that he had led a dissipated life and written some books that were difficult to follow. Supposedly, he had been a genius who had greatly influenced modern philosophy and psychology outside of Denmark. But I had only a vague idea of exactly why and how this was. And since I had grown up in a conservative, pietistic subculture that never mentioned Kierkegaard or even believed that this squandering philosopher could possibly have been a true Christian, I had never really cared about anything he had had to say.

KØBENHAVNS BYMUSEUM

I saw a pair of reading glasses, a pipe and some other things in a glass case. There were a couple of paintings on the wall, a rosewood bookcase and a chair. The set of his collected works amounted to about 13,000 pages. A note informed me that Kierkegaard had written the bulk of it within a period of approximately six years. I was impressed.

But what impressed me most was a mahogany writing desk, a secretary in front of which the philosopher had stood, writing most of those pages. I walked up to the secretary and tried to imagine what it must have felt like to be a writer of such stature and energy. And as I stood at the very same spot where the genius had stood 150 years earlier, pouring out his heart through his pointed pen, something odd happened to me. I felt as if, for a fraction of a second, I had stepped into his body and mind, leaving my own behind, and I experienced a strange, melancholic rush of creative energy that I knew was not my own. At first I felt frightened, then I bowed my head and began to pray, arms resting on the secretary. The world disappeared, and the secretary and I floated off as I held on, just as Elijah must have held on to his chariot of fire. But unlike Elijah, I landed back on earth, at 10:21 a.m., to be exact. It was beginning to snow outside, the way it usually snows in Denmark, with huge, wet snowflakes that disappear as soon as they hit the ground. I left the museum with my umbrella and disappeared into the crowd.

I felt as if, for a fraction of a second, I had stepped into his body and mind, leaving my own behind, and I experienced a strange, melancholic rush of creative energy that I knew was not my own. At first I felt frightened, then I bowed my head and began to pray, arms resting on the secretary.

When I returned to Oregon, I brought with me several of Kierkegaard's books. They lay open all over my apartment like travel guides directing me toward a journey I knew I must take. In the next months I crossed vast plains within my soul and discovered new landscapes of my spirit. My mind was ready to recognize what I read, and my heart was hungry to accept it. I both hit the bottom of anxiety and despair, and climbed to peak experiences of pure joy and peace. As the journey continued and I was forced to confront some of the darkest corners of my soul, I realized a new kind of light shining from the eternal shore. Through this process of anxiety and despair my spirit was eventually healed, my past redeemed, and my future was restored. From having been an enemy I wanted to conquer, suffering now became a friend by which I was learning to conquer myself.

One of the things this initial encounter with Kierkegaard taught me was that there are no shortcuts to an authentic, Christian life. Anxiety, doubt and despair will always be our companions as long as we are conscious of who we are but trying to be something else, or something less. God created us with a nature yearning to be fulfilled in the purpose it envisions. True joy is lived according to the yearnings of the soul. We are all born in sin, and life can only be what God meant it to be through the process of our becoming spirit, an authentic personality, an original self. In Kierkegaard's words, we can only be truly human through the process of becoming. In order to overcome anxiety and despair we must become "a single individual" by constantly choosing to be ourselves, not somebody else. This is the privilege, the freedom and responsibility of every creature created in the image of God. This will cost us everything, eventually ourselves. "Only when a man has become so unhappy, or has grasped the misery of his existence so profoundly that he can truly say, 'For me life is worthless,'" says Kierkegaard, "only then can life have worth in the highest degree."

The following year I was asked to prepare a book about Kierkegaard for an international, evangelical market. I was both thrilled and scared about the project and returned to Copenhagen to do the research. I spent most of the summer of 1996 in the Royal Library of Copenhagen and the Søren Kierkegaard Library

> *In order to overcome anxiety and despair we must become "a single individual" by constantly choosing to be ourselves, not somebody else.*

at the University of Copenhagen. I also attended some lectures at the Kierkegaard conference at the University of Copenhagen, the first such gathering of international scholars in 41 years. The people I met both during the conference and at the Søren Kierkegaard Research Center and the Søren Kierkegaard Society were extremely helpful, and some of them have contributed to this book.

Kierkegaard is experiencing quite a renaissance in the 1990s. This decade is similar to the 1840s, when Kierkegaard wrote his philosophy of life. Today, as then, and as in the 1930s when Kierkegaard was first "discovered" by the French existentialists, we live in a time of mass movements and politics of the masses, when the individual is isolated and lonely and hardly counts. Writers and artists, as well as the international film industry, are being influenced by Kierkegaard's existential thinking. Movie after movie has been released in which Kierkegaard's point of view is unmistakable, movies ranging from *Amadeus* to *Groundhog Day*.

Nonetheless, Kierkegaard's existential philosophy can only be understood if seen in the light of his religious experiences and devout Christian faith. This side of Kierkegaard has often been overlooked by his modern admirers in their attempt to demythologize him because they have not experienced for themselves the depth of religious conditions for sin, repentance, conversion and grace that helped shape Kierkegaard's philosophy. On the other hand, Kierkegaard's Christian message can only be understood correctly in the shadow of his philosophy of what it means to be human. They are like two hands joined together. Evangelical Christians should have a fair chance to understand both, and I leave it to them to judge for themselves the totality of Kierkegaard's philosophy.

This book is a popular introduction to a complicated Christian thinker. It does not do full justice to his deeper philosophical and psychological studies, but, in the spirit of Kierkegaard, I hope that it does confront the reader with himself and his God, inspiring an even deeper exploration of the works only briefly mentioned here. ■

> *Kierkegaard's existential philosophy can only be understood if seen in the light of his religious experiences and devout Christian faith.*

Christianity – A Message About Existence

That is why each generation must start on it anew.

The two most glaring misinterpretations concerning Christianity are:

1. Christianity is not a doctrine (but then the mischief about orthodoxy cropped up, bringing with it various quarrels, so that even while people's lives remained entirely unchanged, they bickered about what is Christian in the same way that Platonic philosophy is argued about.) — Christianity is a message about existence. That is why each generation must start on it anew; the accumulated erudition of preceding generations is essentially superfluous, yet not to be scorned as long as this generation understands itself and its limits, but extremely dangerous if it does not.

2. Since Christianity is not a doctrine, it is not a matter of indifference, as in the case of a doctrine, <u>who</u> is expounding it as long as the one doing so (objectively) says the right thing. No, Christ did not appoint professors, but followers. If Christianity (precisely because it is not a doctrine) is not reduplicated in the life of the person expounding it, then he does not expound Christianity, for Christianity is a message about living and can only be expounded by its realization in men's lives. Altogether, living in it,

> "Christ did not appoint professors, but followers.

expressing Christianity in one's life, etc., is what it means to reduplicate. . . .

To reduplicate is to be what one professes. Therefore people are infinitely better off with someone who does not speak too loftily, but is what he professes to be. I have never been bold enough to say that the world is evil. I make this discrimination: Christianity teaches that the world is evil. But I dare not say so; I am far from being pure enough myself to say that. But I have said: the world is mediocre, and that is just what my own life expresses. But how many milksop parsons stand in their pulpits thundering about the world being evil – and what, I wonder, do their lives express? – I have never been bold enough to say that I would risk everything for the sake of Christianity. I am not yet that strong. I begin in a smaller way. I know that I have risked a good deal, and I think and believe that God will educate me so that I may learn to risk more.

Journals 1848

Kierkegaard usually refused to pose for pictures. Therefore most portraits of him were drawn after his death (including the painting on the cover of this book). The portrait above is painted by Leyah Jensen, an American highschool student.

"*I know that I have risked a good deal, and I believe that God will educate me so that I may learn to risk more.*"

11

The Crucial Thing

"What I really need is to get clear about what I must do, not what I must know, except insofar as knowledge must precede every act. What matters is to find a purpose, to see what it really is that God wills that I shall do; the crucial thing is to find a truth which is truth for me, to find the idea for which I am willing to live and die. Of what use would it be to me to discover a so-called objective truth, to work through the philosophical systems so that I could, if asked, make critical judgments about them, could point out the fallacies in each system; of what use would it be to me to be able to develop a theory of the state, getting details from various sources and combining them into a whole, and constructing a world I did not live in but merely held up for others to see; of what use would it be to me to be able to formulate the meaning of Christianity, to be able to explain many specific points — if it had no deeper meaning for me and for my life? . . . I certainly do not deny that I still accept an imperative of knowledge and that through it men may be influenced, but then it must come alive in me, and this is what I now recognize as the most important of all. This is what my soul thirsts for as the African deserts thirst for water. . . . But in order to find that idea — or, to put it more correctly — to find myself, it does no good to plunge still farther into the world. . . ."

Journals, Gilleleje, August 1, 1835

"My purpose in life would seem to be to present the truth as I discover it in such a way as simultaneously to destroy all possible authority."

Journals 1843

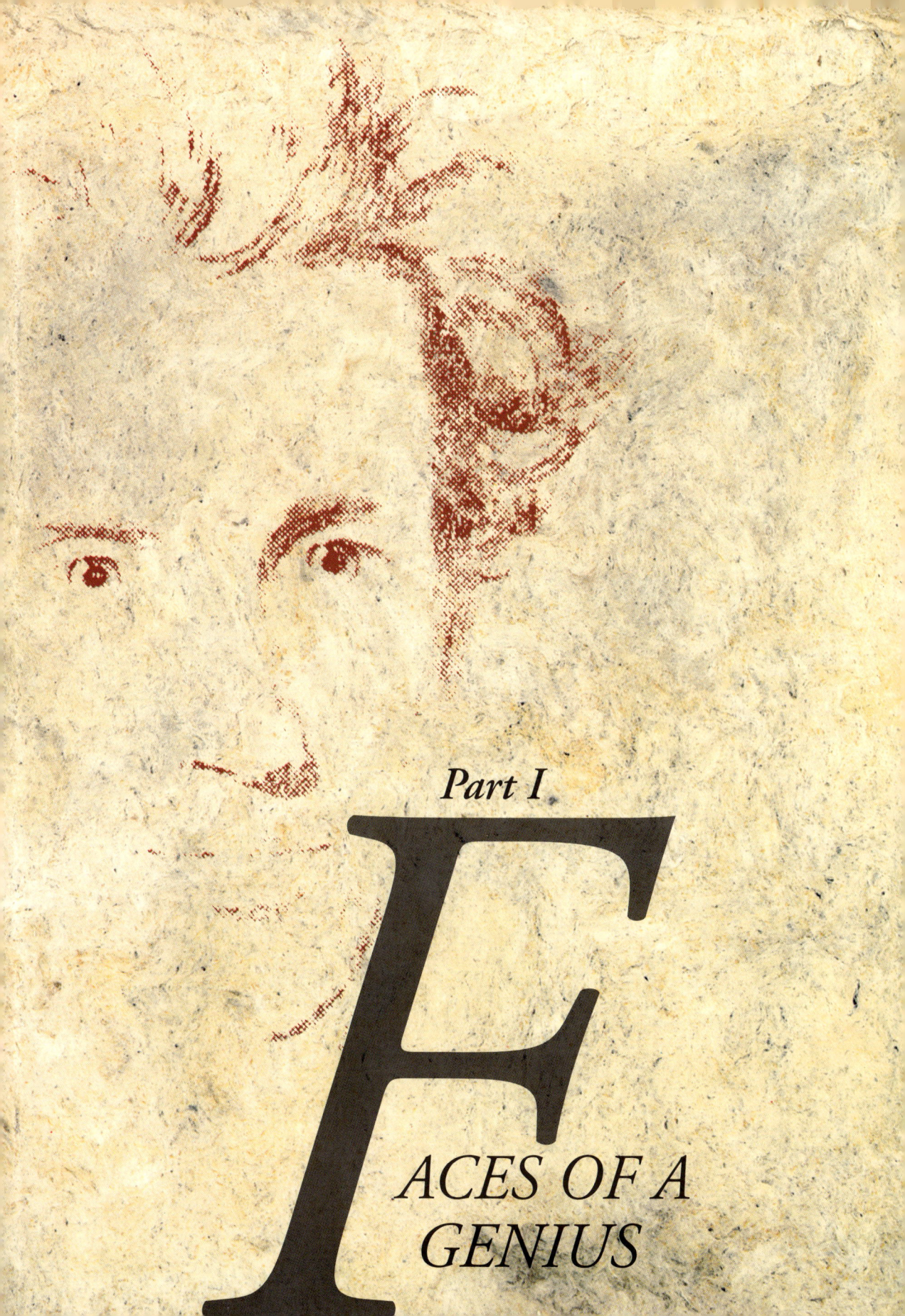

Part I

FACES OF A GENIUS

Kierkegaard's short and rather uneventful life was characterized by a rare dedication to a specific idea, a hard and passionate pursuit of an eternal truth, a quest by which we as his readers may measure our own. From his early youth as a theology student at the University of Copenhagen, until the day he collapsed on a street and lay dying in Frederiksberg Hospital, Kierkegaard wrestled with the meaning of human existence in the light of Christian faith. Few thinkers have plunged deeper into the abyss of the soul to expose the depravity of man, and no believer has soared higher in search of human glory. Kierkegaard was a primary contributor in shaping 20th-century philosophical and theological attitudes. Many concepts and insights taken for granted today, ideas that permeate modern ways of thinking, were first discovered and explained by "the melancholic Dane," a man with the courage to scrutinize the landscape of his own precarious existence. He dared to do this despite suffering countless misunderstandings and outright ridicule at the hands of his contemporaries. Kierkegaard was a prophet of pain, a provocateur of possibility, a genius living a century ahead of his time, a struggling Christian who defied wrong answers and managed to raise some right and crucial questions. In this he was willing to judge himself more harshly than he ever judged others.

This does not however, mean that the potential of Kierkegaard's ideas has been exhausted, or that his message has fully been absorbed into modern ways of thinking. On the contrary. The surface of what he had to say has barely been scratched, and sad to say, half the lesson has yet to be learned. The present, as then, is a time of bulletproof systems, easy-to-apply directions and how-to answers and substitutes, all threatening to undermine human freedom and personal responsibility. As Malcolm Muggeridge wrote in an *Observer* article on January 1, 1967, Kierkegaard "continually points out, all that is most mediocre and contemptible in human beings derives from the pursuit of earthly happiness. It is the glory of Christianity to have denounced and defied this pursuit; the Christian who nonetheless goes crawling on his stomach to make his peace with happiness earns Kierkegaard's particular contempt."

Kierkegaard demonstrates that life's purpose is not necessarily to become happy, at least not in the secure and bourgeois sense of the word. The meaning of life, that which makes life happy, is to find one's particular purpose, to will that

> *Few thinkers have plunged deeper into the abyss of the soul to expose the depravity of man, and no believer has soared higher in search of human glory.*

14

one thing which constitutes purity of heart, and to become a person capable of carrying out that idea. This always hurts, both inwardly and outwardly, since a person who follows through an idea in his heart is, and always will be, essentially unpopular. But this is precisely what Christ calls each of us to be: individuals with a mission for which we are willing to live and die. To be a Christian does not mean to progress in optimism, but to regress through suffering to the point of despair where an absurd leap of faith is the only possible escape to joy.

The genius of Kierkegaard is that whereas he exposes mediocrity and calls for an authentic, Christian existence by promoting the truth, he also renounces every claim to authority by bringing us into a disparity from which we can only be rescued if we absorb the truth ourselves. "Only that person is mature who absorbs truth and makes it his own," he said, adding, "I can never force a person to an opinion, a conviction, a faith. But one thing I can do . . . I can force him to become aware" (*The Point of View*, 1848).

Kierkegaard chose to take advantage of his unhappy destiny by stepping outside the State Church system and attacking it from there. This was the only logical way. For anyone who sets out to challenge an authoritative, dogmatic system has no choice but to propose the alternative in a provocative and hypothetical form. Otherwise he will only be adding new wine to old wineskins.

It is amazing that the voice of this modern John the Baptist was not recognized in the English-speaking world until almost a hundred years after his death. When his works were finally translated, first into German and French, then English, he emerged from the subconscious of an era and his works had a stunning impact. Here were the ideas which a disillusioned world needed in order to understand what was going on in the 20th century. And here was a personal key for every thinking individual, whether Christian, Buddhist or atheist, capable of unlocking the door to the future. Kierkegaard's ideas had a major influence on existential philosophy, psychology, and neoorthodox theology — trends that changed our concepts and the way we understand reality today.

We may study Kierkegaard's philosophy of life, and thereby discover a direction for our own. But if in the process, we do not discover ourselves and the specific purpose for which we ourselves are willing to live and die, we have misread him. We may become purely "Kierkegaardian," we may be able to decipher the most cryptic of his writings and explain his most difficult concepts, but unless we first of all become aware of ourselves and the specific purpose of God in our own lives, all is in vain; we are only, as Kierkegaard said, like "schoolboys who cheat their teacher by copying the answer out of a book, without having worked it out for themselves." ■

> *The meaning of life, that which makes life happy, is to find one's particular purpose, to will that one thing which constitutes purity of heart, and to become a person capable of carrying out that idea.*

The University of Copenhagen with Our Lady's Cathedral behind, in 1840 (left) and 1996 (right). Kierkegaard studied theology, literature, philosophy and science here for ten years, until he finally decided to finish his theological degree.

" There once lived a father and a son. They were both very gifted and witty, especially the father. . . . Once in a while the father would look at the son and see how troubled he was, then he would say, "Poor boy, you're going about in quiet despair. . . ." Besides that no word was ever mentioned about the matter. But within the memory of man this father and son may have been the two most melancholic beings who ever lived. . . . And the father thought that the son's melancholy was his fault, and the son believed that the father's melancholy was his fault, and so they never spoke to each other about it.

Journals 1844

Søren Kierkegaard's father, *Michael Pedersen Kierkegaard* (1756-1838), grew up among poor farmers in Sædding in western Jutland. When he was twelve he went to work for his uncle who was a merchant in Copenhagen. At the age of twenty-four he established his own business, and for the next sixteen years he ran it so successfully that he was able to invest a fortune in bonds and retire when he was forty. His wife Kirstine died childless after two years of marriage, and within a year after her death Michael married his housekeeper Ane who was by then already several months pregnant. Their first daughter was born in 1797. Then followed two more daughters and four sons, of whom Søren was the youngest.

Søren and Michael had a close relationship. Michael was eager to shape little Søren's personality, and he did a thorough job. In actual fact, he ruled his favorite son while alive and later from the grave to such an extent that Søren said he sometimes felt like a chained galley slave.

Nonetheless, Søren's early years were mostly happy. There were times when Michael would take his favorite child by the hand and walk across the living room floor while pretending they were taking a walk in the busy street outside. Michael would talk about imaginary sights, pointing out obstacles, greeting people, exchanging remarks and so on, until Søren finally felt so exhausted that he had to rest. At other times, Michael would allow Søren to overhear intellectual discussions among the adults. These were times when Michael would encourage his opponent to make his point as clearly as possible while he patiently listened. Then Michael would respond and reverse the argument. The discussion would continue for hours, like a chess game where each move is new and surprising. From his chair behind them Søren would watch it all, entranced by the pros and cons of dialectical discussion, and when his father would finally present the argument which asserted the supremacy of his position, Søren felt a thrill run up his spine. Sometimes late at night, Michael would pull out a set of picture cards with past heroes like William Tell or Napoleon and tell Søren stories about them. Then Michael would turn suddenly grave, pull out a picture of the crucified Christ, and tell about how God had suffered on the

I was born in 1813, in that mad year when so many other mad banknotes were put into circulation, and I can be best compared to one of them. There is something about me which points to greatness, but because of the mad state of affairs I am only worth little. Journals

Why didn't I grow up like other children, why wasn't I wrapped in joy, why did I so early have to gaze into the realm of sighs, why was I born with an inborn anxiety which continuously let me face it, why was nine months in my mother's womb enough to make me old so I was born not as a child but as an old man? Journals

Søren's childhood home at Nytorv in Copenhagen. The house was located next to the courthouse (behind tree).

18

cross in order to save people from their terrible sins. "Make sure, Søren, that you truly love our Lord Jesus Christ," he said as he turned out the light, and Søren would be left alone in the dark.

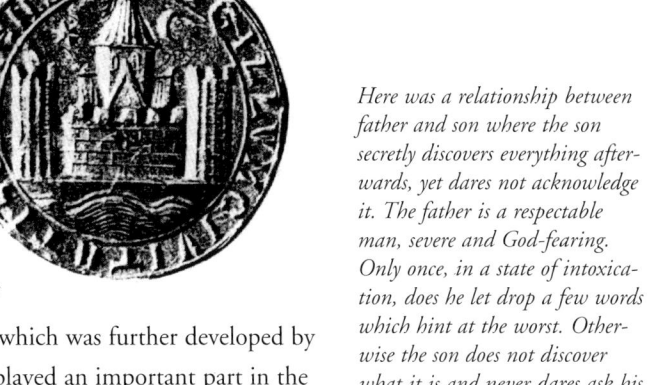

Søren inherited three major dispositions from his father: a vivid imagination, a strong sense of dialectics and logic, and a dark, religious melancholy which was further developed by the Moravian church Michael attended. Each aspect played an important part in the development of Søren's psyche, leaving him ambivalent about his father's effect on him. Later in life he sometimes praised his father; at other times he mourned a cruel upbringing during which his father had forced his own religious moods and troubles onto Søren with no regard for the child's sensibility. At some point, when Søren was around twenty-two and his father was close to eighty, Michael must have hinted at something in his past which made Søren realize a possible reason for his father's unspoken despair and the dismal atmosphere at home. The father's confession might have referred to his premarital relationship with Ane, for Søren makes a reference to King David's wealth and spiritual despair as a punishment for his sexual misconduct in *Stages On Life's Way*, which he wrote shortly after the journal entry of 1844. But the "great earthquake," Søren's full realization of the consequences of his father's sins, an awareness that his father's depression might be due to a curse called upon the family by the father, only occurred when Ane and five of the children had passed away and Søren's father was almost eighty. At that point Michael finally unburdened his heart to Søren, leaving his son in a profound state of shock and confusion, since his confession not only revealed secret sins from the past, but also made Søren realize that Christianity did not necessarily bring forgiveness and peace of heart, even to a believer as serious and conscientious as his father. Søren probably promised his father never to reveal his secret to anyone, but at the same time he took offence at his "stuffy, Christian faith." He needed some fresh air, freedom from "the spiritual stays" in which his father had kept him, so for a while he sought the pleasures of the world. "It is the same with Christianity or with becoming a Christian as it is with all radical cures. One postpones it as long as possible," he wrote October 9, 1835. He turned to philosophy, natural sciences, politics, literature, theater, pleasure and parties — anything that could distract him from the gloom of his father's pious faith and along the lines of which he could exercise his awakening intellectual gifts. His Christian faith had shipwrecked, it simply made no sense anymore. He moved out on his own, visited bars frequently, and perhaps even a brothel, and he worked himself into debt. For eighteen months he threw himself into the kind of self-indulgence he would later characterize as an aesthetic lifestyle. Not until the spring of 1838 did he come to his

Here was a relationship between father and son where the son secretly discovers everything afterwards, yet dares not acknowledge it. The father is a respectable man, severe and God-fearing. Only once, in a state of intoxication, does he let drop a few words which hint at the worst. Otherwise the son does not discover what it is and never dares ask his father or others about it. Journals 1844.

Then it was that the great earthquake occurred, the terrible revolution which suddenly forced upon me a new and infallible law of interpretation of all the facts. At that point I suspected that my father's great age was not a divine blessing, but rather a curse. . . . A guilt must fall upon the whole family, the punishment of God must be on it; it was to disappear, wiped out by the powerful hand of God, obliterated like an unsuccessful attempt, and only at times did I find some little relief in the thought that my father had been allotted the heavy task of calming us with the consolation of religion. . . . Journals 1838

I grew up . . . in orthodoxy; but as soon as I began to think for myself the tremendous colossus began to totter. I call it a colossus with purpose, for taken as a whole it is very consistent and in the course of centuries the different parts have fused so tightly together that it is difficult to quarrel with it. I could of course agree with it on certain points, but these would have to be treated like shoots, found in the cracks of a rock. On the other hand, I could also see what was wrong with it at many different points, but I had to leave the fundamentals in dubio for a time. Journals, June 1, 1835

senses and experience a kind of ethical conversion. "If Christ is to come and take up His abode in me," he wrote in his journal on April 22, "it must happen according to the title of today's Gospel in the almanac: Christ came in through locked doors." A month later he celebrated a joyous return to the Christian faith by taking Holy Communion and reconciling with his aging father. He moved back home, and a few weeks later Michael died. "I had so very much wished that he might live a few years longer, and I look upon his death as the last sacrifice which he made to his love for me; for he did not die from me but *died for me* in order that if possible I might still turn into something," he wrote in the journal on August 11, 1838. Søren considered Michael's death an atoning sacrifice, and the sacrifice helped him make up his mind to leave the world behind and finally finish his theological studies. A pastorate in the State Church was within his grasp. But first he wanted to pay a visit to the place in western Jutland where his father had grown up. ■

Twelve–year–old Michael Curses God

Out on the moors . . . a young boy was tending his sheep. . . . The frightened boy had many strange thoughts about the Lord up in His blue heaven.

Actually, he was scared of Him. It was better to be on good terms with God, otherwise He might grow angry just like the giant from the North Sea. Sometimes He could even become so furious with humans and their evil ways, that no one in Sædding parish knew how to appease Him. He just sat in heaven on a throne of sun-fire and watched what everyone in the parish did. Should a farmer dare to forget about His providence, then his peace in this world would swiftly be over.

The shepherd boy feared God on high, but he did not love him. How could God allow a poor boy to be alone on the moors with no shelter or a place to hide? . . . The good Lord sat in His golden skies knowing about a boy tending sheep in Ringkøbing county. He knew very well how this boy often suffered from heat or cold, of sadness and dread. He knew very well that a barefoot boy on earth often prayed that his flock might be taken from him. . . .

But to what use was a shepherd boy's protests if even a farmer in Sædding could not insist on his right before God? What difference would a boy's complaints make if even Lars Kresten's wife, who had been bedridden for fifteen years without being able to move, had not had her prayers answered?

The shepherd boy sat among his mute sheep while the rain poured down. It was another three hours until supper and he would have to stay, for his father was a strict man who would become angry if his sheep came home early just because of the rain. . . . At some point the boy burst into tears, but after a while he stopped. No one cared about a shepherd boy's cries. Pained by dread and sadness he walked across the moor and climbed a hill covered with heather. When he reached the top he looked around on all sides to make sure no one was watching him. . . . Then he clenched his cold fists, turned his swollen face toward the dark sky, raised his arms in a threatening gesture at a silent and angry God and cursed Him.

"I hate You up there!" he yelled, hurling a child's curses against an implacable God, pouring out his misery before God's throne, even while the wind and rain kept whipping his pale and angry face. . . . Then he went down the hill, and one hour later he walked back to the farm with his sheep. ■ (Svend Leopold, *Søren Kierkegaard: Geniets tragedie,* Gyldendal, Copenhagen 1932)

20

A Visit to Sædding
Interview with Anders Stengaard

The secret sin which haunted Michael Pedersen Kierkegaard with guilt and gloom, a hybris which made Søren wonder whether he was under a family curse, goes back to Michael's childhood in western Jutland. Before his death, Michael confided in Søren that he, as a twelve-year-old shepherd boy on the moors of Sædding, had once cursed God. In 1840, after his father's death and with his theological exams behind him, Kierkegaard decided to make a "pilgrimage" to his father's birthplace. Today, more than 150 years later, a local farmer and distant relative of Kierkegaard, Anders Stengaard, explains:

"Søren Kierkegaard visited Sædding only once, in 1840 after his father Michael died. I guess Søren felt he owed it to Michael to see the place he had so often heard him talk about. The trip lasted three or four weeks. As he was traveling there by stagecoach, Søren wrote in his journal, 'I'm sitting here counting the hours till I shall see Sædding. I want to see the places where he as a poor boy tended sheep, those places I have felt homesick for because of him.' Søren even imagined that he might die during this visit and be buried in the local cemetery. In the same entry he recalls his father lovingly, 'From him I learned what fatherly love is, and through his love I realized the reality of God's fatherly love, the only unshakable thing in life, the true archimedean point.'

"Søren arrived on a Sunday and stayed three days with his Aunt Else. He must have enjoyed the landscape and the simple folk around him — at least he gives this emotional description of the place, 'To stand outside the gate of the little farmhouse in the late evening light when the sheep are driven home and dark clouds send flashes of light which forecast strong winds, to see the moor rising in the background! I wish I could always keep with me the memory of this evening.'"

Anders pauses and pulls out a penciled sketch from his pocket. "I drew this picture of Søren and Aunt Else."

> *Michael grew up in a pietistic family influenced by the German Herrnhuters. His conscience was deeply rooted in a strong awareness of sin and guilt, and he never forgot this hubris in cursing God.*

Left (top): This stone has been erected on the field where Michael's family farm once stood.
Right (top): Sædding Church.
Right (bottom): Anders' drawing of Søren and Aunt Else.

This mysterious face can be seen on the nothern wall of Sædding Church.

Anders walks across the country road and points at a huge boulder which marks the location of Kierkegaard's family home. The Sædding church rises in the background, together with patches of moor left untouched by the plow. Anders points to a hill across the field. "This might very well be the place where Michael cursed God when he was twelve. He regretted it for the rest of his life, and that remorse may have contributed to his melancholic moods. Michael grew up in a pietistic family influenced by the German Herrnhuters. His conscience was deeply rooted in a strong awareness of sin and guilt, and he never forgot this hubris in cursing God. At some point he must have shared his feelings of guilt with Søren. Søren's journal alludes to 'a great earthquake' when his father supposedly confessed his past sins and secrets to him. It was no doubt a shocking experience for Søren, and for the rest of his life he believed he had inherited the consequences of his father's guilt. This may be the reason why he was unable to marry Regine. He simply could not bear to pass on his suffering to her. At the same time, it may also have roused his genius and helped shape his vision. In one of his Christian discourses from 1848, Søren Kierkegaard talked about the joy of attaining that affliction as being a special kind of success in its own right: 'What is success? Success is what helps me reach my goal, or what leads me to my goal. . . . Even if the road that leads you to your goal is the hardest of all, it is success. . . . Do you think that a poet, whose songs bring joy to humanity, could have written his songs without having his soul tuned in through affliction and diverse adversity? . . . At first, the poet may have found it heavy, even gruesome, that his soul had to be tormented in order to bring comfort to others.'"

Anders pauses and climbs the hill. To the east, the moor stretches as far as the eye can see. A tree turns its back on the west wind. A dog is barking far away. Fog rolls in from the ocean. An entry from Kierkegaard's journal, written amidst this barren landscape more than 150 years ago, comes to mind: "The heath must be especially influential in developing strong minds; here all lies naked, bared before God, and here the multifarious diversions have no place, the many odd nooks and crannies in which our minds can hide and whence it is often hard for serious purpose to collect the scattered thoughts. Here the mind must close in upon itself, definately and exactingly. 'Whither shall I flee from Thy presence?' one could ask in truth here on the heath." *(Journals, July-August 1840)* ■

Top: "This might very well be the place where Michael cursed God when he was twelve."
Bottom: Interior of Sædding Church (12th century).

"**Besides my numerous circle of acquaintances with whom, by and large, I maintain very super- ficial relations, I have one close confidante – my melancholy – and in the midst of my rejoicing, in the midst of my work, she waves to me, beckons me to her side and I go to her, even though my physical frame stays in place; she is the most faithful mistress I have known; what wonder then that I, on my part, must be ready to follow her in an instant.**

Journals 1841

On his return from Sædding, Søren Kierkegaard was eager to see a certain girl by the name of Regine Olsen, the daughter of Councillor of State Terkel Olsen. Regine was an attractive and cheerful seventeen-year-old whom Kierkegaard had met three years earlier. Before his departure for western Jutland, he had let her borrow some books. This gave him an excuse to see her again when he returned. Søren fell in love with Regine and decided to propose to her. With his *Sturm und Drang* period behind him, and a theological degree that would qualify him for a pastorate in the State Church, he was ready to marry and have a family. Regine would be the perfect match, he felt.

One month after his return, Kierkegaard made a stormy proposal which took Regine by surprise. At first, she was dumbfounded by his awkward and passionate attempts, but Søren was persistent. He went directly to her father and asked for his daughter's hand. Two days later father and daughter accepted the proposal. Søren and Regine became engaged.

Only days after the engagement was made official, however, Søren became convinced that it was a mistake. He realized that the romance could not lift the cloud of gloom and deep-seated somberness which he had inherited from his father, and he could not bear to place the innocent girl he loved under the "curse" which hovered over him and his family, a secret which he had promised never to reveal to anyone. But to break an engagement in those days was a serious matter which would both humiliate the girl and her family, as well as bring scandal onto Kierkegaard. So instead he pretended to maintain the romance while at the same time, doing what he could to make her initiate the break. But Regine held on. She had come to love Søren and simply refused to let him go.

A year went by, during which Søren grew certain that there could never be a happy ending. Not only did he desperately want to save her from the consequences of his depression, indeed as much as she wanted to save him from it. But he had also come to realize that the incompatibilities which had previously seemed only minor, were in fact major obstacles for a deeper union between them. Regine was not reflective enough and lacked the spiritual depth needed by a man like Kierkegaard. In

Thou empress of my heart ("Regina'), treasured in the deepest fastness of my breast, in the fullness of my thought, there, where it is equally far to heaven and to hell - unknown divinity! Oh, can I really believe the past tales, that when one first sees the object of one's love, one imagines one has seen her long ago, that all love like all knowledge is remembrance, that love too has its prophecies in the individual, its types, its myths, its Old Testament.
Journals, February 2, 1839

On September 8 I left my house with the firm purpose of deciding the matter. We met each other in the street outside their house. She said thare was nobody at home. I was foolhardy enough to look upon that as an invitation, just the opportunity I wanted. I went in with her. We stood alone in the living room. She was a little uneasy. I asked her to play me something as she usually did. She did so; but that did not help me. Then suddenly I took the music away and closed it, not without a certain violence, threw it down on the piano and said, "Oh, what do I care about music now! It is you I am searching for, it is you whom I have sought after for two years." Journals 1841

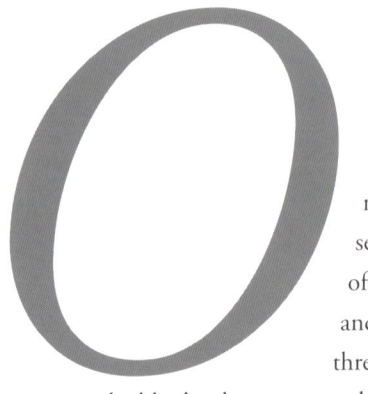

The four ramparts around Copenhagen were the "brim" behind which the Danish capital protected itself against enemies. On Sundays it was a popular place to walk and socialize, and Kierkegaard often caught a glimpse of Regine here without being able to talk to her and explain why he had had to break off the engagement. Instead, he wrote three major books about it.

Today, only the southern rampart remains; Copenhagen has long since spilled over its brim.

August of 1841 he returned the engagement ring with a short letter in which he tried to convince her that he would never be able to make her happy. But Regine pleaded, so Søren agreed to put the ring back on and give their relationship a second chance. Outwardly it looked as if the crisis were over, but Søren was actually getting ready for a final break. For the time being he put Regine on hold as he finished his doctoral thesis *On the Concept of Irony*, which he defended successfully on September 29th, 1841. Later that day he walked to Regine's home and broke the engagement only two months after his first attempt. Then he went to see a play at the Royal Theater. During the intermission, Regine's father arrived and tried to talk him out of his decision. Søren agreed to eat supper with the Olsen family, but the next day he made one last final break with Regine, then went home and cried himself to sleep. The farce was over, this was positively the last performance, and he had no intention of staying for the reviews in a small, provincial town hungry for scandals. Søren decided to exit to Berlin, together with his suitcase full of notes from which he hoped to write a book. ■

The next day I saw that I had made a false step. A penitent such as I was, my vita ante acta, my melancholy, that was enough. I suffered unspeakably at that time. Journals 1841

This is the curse brooding over me, never to dare to let any human being be seriously tied to me. . . . To make it easier for her I would like to make her believe I am a simple deceiver, a reckless person, in order to make her hate me; for I think it might be much harder for her if she sensed it was melancholy. Journals 1841

From that moment I dedicated my life with every ounce of my poor ability to the service of an idea. Journals

*Left page: Regine, Søren's fiancée.
Right page (left): Holmens Church where Søren was baptized and the couple sometimes went to church.
Right page (bottom): Same view at Kierkegaard's time. The building with the steeple was the stock exchange, Børsen.
Right page (right): The "Six Sisters" behind Børsen where Regine's family lived.*

Working on Love

Interview with Pia Søltoft

Pia Søltoft is currently a Ph.D. stipendiary at the Søren Kierkegaard Research Center. Since 1993, when she earned her master's degree in theology, she has been teaching theology at the University of Copenhagen.

You are working on a Ph.D. based on Kierkegaard's ethics, more specifically the connection between subjectivity and inter-subjectivity. What does that mean?

I am looking at Kierkegaard's concept of subjectivity, trying to see what the connection between the individual and his neighbor does to this concept. When we talk about individuality in Kierkegaard, we usually think of being oneself alone in front of God. What I am studying are the ethical implications, the relationship and responsibility one has to other people. According to Kierkegaard, this kind of responsibility is not just for the good of the other person. He is of course the real object, but it also has a reciprocal effect on the self, thereby determining it to some extent. The self cannot be itself alone, it needs a social context in order to stay itself. This is what the phrase inter-subjectivity alludes to.

Could you explain what Kierkegaard says about this in Works of Love?

Works of Love is a complex book in which Kierkegaard discusses love for one's neighbor, while also addressing the love shared between two people. He tries to combine the two by claiming that in order to have love for one's neighbor, a person must see through and change the normal love relationship between two people. This change will happen by means of a third party involved in the relationship. For love to be truly complete, one must have the love between the lover and the beloved, plus what Kierkegaard calls Love, or simply God. Love of one's neighbor consists of a union between these three. Most of *Works of Love* is a series of analyses of what goes wrong in a love relationship. Kierkegaard says that the basic prob-

> The self cannot be a self alone, it needs a social context.

lem here is that most kinds of love are really just an attempt to leave out the other person, rather than trying to love the other person for who he is. It is really a kind of self-love. In a love relationship, for instance, the way you prefer the other person tells more about your love for *yourself* *in* the other person than it does about your love for him or her. And if you only love yourself in another person, you don't see that other person at all. The reason for your love is only self-fulfillment. This kind of love is a love of preference, a way of loving him because he is loveable, for what he can offer you. This has some negative implications, and in order to change these implications there has to be a third party, what Kierkegaard calls Love, or God. To include this third party opens the relationship up, so that instead of loving yourself in the other, you see the other person in his concreteness. This means that you see in him the likeness of God, while also still seeing that he is different from you - he is *him*self, not *your* other self. You are able to distinguish between your love and your own expectations. This is the whole purpose of *Works of Love*: to open up the relationship and raise it to a higher, less self-centered level where basic relationships between people will become all they were meant to be.

Does this mean that there cannot be love between two people unless they believe in God?

> *Kierkegaard says that the basic problem here is that most kinds of love are really just an attempt to leave out the other person, rather than trying to love the other person for who he is. It is really a kind of self-love.*

Not necessarily. In fact, Kierkegaard says a lot of positive things about our inborn urge to love, how love is a basic power that connects people as friends, lovers, neighbors and so on. But there is always a danger in such a relationship, the danger of self-love. Many have misread *Works of Love* by suggesting that Kierkegaard's view of love between man and woman is negative. If they were right, Kierkegaard would have a problem. But that is not the case. Kierkegaard doesn't make any judgments here, he just tries to analyze relationships among people, while pointing out the dangers of self-love.

How can one become aware of the quality of one's love?
You cannot see it with the eye by just watching the relationship. You will have to turn to yourself and discern the motives driving you. Only then will you be able to discern what is going on in a relationship.

Satirical drawing by Wilhelm Marstrand portraying Kierkegaard as the "seducer."

Does Kierkegaard provide a "self-test" for lovers?
The last section in *Works of Love* is called "Recollecting One Who Is Dead." This chapter is often considered morbid and nonsocial,

but what it really does is provide a key for testing love. Kierkegaard suggests you pretend to go to the grave of the one you love and remember this person. If your love does not change, then you have passed the test. The dead person is not able to change or ask for love, so if, in your imagination, your love is the same as when that person was alive, it proves that your love is unselfish because it holds the other as the object of your love rather than yourself. This test is a thought experiment, of course, which you may apply at any point in a relationship. Kierkegaard is not talking about being faithful to the dead but about being faithful to the living present in one's life. *Works of Love* is a tremendous tool for accomplishing just that.

Kierkegaard has often been misinterpreted as an advocate of self-realization and irresponsible individualism. Does he seem to offer a better way in Works of Love?
Yes. For Kierkegaard, a relationship is something between an *I* and a *Thou*, between two different, yet equal people. Most often, however, relationships are made up of two I's who see only themselves reflected in the other. Kierkegaard does not propose a romantic, irresponsible individuality. For him, the self cannot be itself alone, it can only be itself in relation to its surroundings which constantly have a reciprocal effect on the self. In order to remain oneself in the world, one must nurture relationships. You cannot *be* yourself once and for all. If a person claims this, he is precisely not himself, and has instead fallen in love with himself. To stay yourself, to maintain the continuity with self, you have to relate to others. The self is not an island, since man is created with the urge to love and only in the fulfillment of this urge can he remain true to himself.

How do you define a Thou?
The basic idea in *Works of Love* is equality between two people, either because of the image of God in them, or, if you prefer, because of the foundation of Love within them. Although on the surface they may have differences, both are unique human beings who must learn to recognize and appreciate their common characteristics, as well as their differences. To want to change a person into becoming like you is to make him into another *I*, but to respect him as a *Thou* is to recognize that he is different from you, and yet alike.

Why do you think that the concept of ethics in general, and Kierkegaard's ethics in particular,

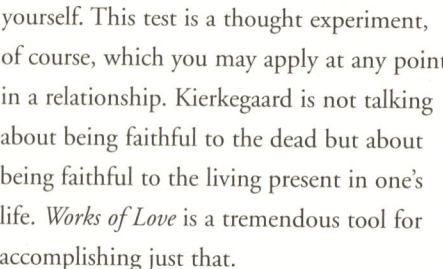

> This is the whole purpose of Works of Love: to open up the relationship and raise it to a higher, less self-centered level where basic relationships among people will become all they were meant to be.

is having a renaissance now, toward the end of the 20th century?

It may be due to the collapse of an age of ideologies when people no longer had systems to rely on. When the Wall fell, it not only signified the end of one of the last major political systems in the world, it also signified the end of ideological absolutes. Ethics is what fills the vacuum in this loss of absolutes, and Kierkegaard's ethics in particular provides a valuable tool for grounding our relationships in the absolute we call Love. ■

The commandment said, "You shall love your neighbor as yourself," but if the commandment is properly understood it also says the opposite: You shall love yourself in the right way. Therefore, if anyone is unwilling to learn from Christianity to love himself in the right way, he cannot love the neighbor either. He can perhaps hold together with another or a few other persons, "through thick and thin," as it is called, but this is by no means loving the neighbor. To love yourself in the right way and to love the neighbor correspond perfectly to one another; fundamentally they are one and the same thing. When the Law's as yourself has wrested from you the self-love that Christianity sadly enough must presuppose to be in every human being, then you have actually learned to love yourself. The Law is therefore: You shall love yourself in the same way as you love your neighbor when you love him as yourself.

Works of Love

Listening to the Silence
Kierkegaard and Nature

Left page: This S. H. Petersen etching of Grib Skov (1820) hung on the wall above Kierkegaard's writing desk. Right page (top): 19th-century map showing Ottevejskrogen in Grib Skov, one of Kierkegaard's favorite spots for meditation. Right page (below): The King's Garden, a public park in Copenhagen.

Silence is the essence of inwardness, of the inner life. . . . But talkativeness is afraid of the silence which reveals its emptiness. The Present Age 1846

There are a number of beautiful, poetic observations of nature sprinkled throughout Kierkegaard's journals, many of which were made during his trips to Grib Skov and Gilleleje. He often visited these places, just north of Copenhagen, whenever he was seeking inspiration for his writing.

Kierkegaard was no romantic pantheist. Contrary to the poets of his day, he was an ethical thinker who clearly distinguished between nature and God, between creation and the Creator. According to Kierkegaard, God cannot be found in nature unless we have first found Him in a personal relationship. He is beyond nature. The only place we can find Him is in inwardness: "He is everywhere in nature, though not literally. Not until the individual goes inside himself (in the act of inwardness) will he become aware and able to see God. . . . For although nature is literally God's work, it is not literally God." (The *Postscript*) Only the individual who has seen God in inwardness is able to experience His presence in nature. Anything else is paganism and romantic idealism.

One of Kierkegaard's very first journal entries reflects just how frustrated and powerless he felt when observing nature: "The reason I cannot truly say that I enjoy nature is that it goes beyond my abilities to comprehend what it is exactly that I enjoy." (*Journals 1834*) However, as the years went by and Kierkegaard grew even more spiritually sensitive, he learned to accept this frustration and enjoy nature as a classroom for higher religious education, a house of God, "a temple not built by human hands." Kierkegaard wrote that the beginning of the religious life is marked by the acceptance of this very frustration. It is the point in time when we stop explaining anxiety away by means of reflection or by merely talking away

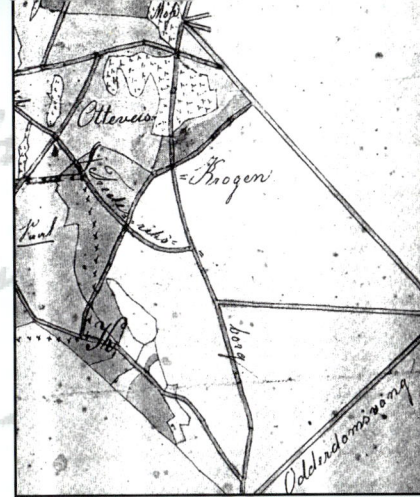

the feeling of nothingness with words. Silence is the beginning of reality, the first step toward infinity. In Kierkegaard's own words, "In the deepest sense you must turn yourself into nothing, become nothing for God, learn to be silent. In this silence rests the starting point." Trusting this silence by opening the soul to nature creates in us the very same qualities as those in nature which glorify the Creator.

In his beautiful discourse, "What we may learn from the lilies of the field and the birds of the air," Kierkegaard shows that silence in nature is the primary condition for humility and obedience:

"Out there with the lily and the bird — there is silence. But this silence, or what we try to learn from it: to become silent — is the first condition for true obedience." (*The Lilies of the Field and the Birds of the Air*)

"From the lily and the bird you will learn to serve

"In contrast to the dark reflection, a flower climbs up and grows on the surface — a nymphæa alba (White Water Lily) which swims around with its big, green leaf: white and pure and innocent it climbs out of the abyss."
Journals 1835

one Master only, to love Him and stay close to Him in everything."

". . . In nature everything is conditioned by obedience. . . . Were there just one star in the sky, or one speck of dust that demanded to have its own way, it would perish right away. For in nature everything is nothing in the way that it is nothing else than an expression of God's unconditional will. As soon as it is not that, it will cease to exist." (Ibid)

Although nature has no choice but to obey, this is what

Houses and the harbor of Gilleleje fishing village on the northern coast of the Danish island Sjælland.

distinguishes it from man. Man is spirit. He is not driven by instincts, he is drawn by longings toward an eternal shore; he can choose whether to obey or not. From this longing and freedom stems both his anxiety and glory, and he will not find ultimate rest until his longing is satisfied in God: "The bird is not seeking anything. However far it flies, it is not seeking: it is migrating and is drawn, and its longest flight is a migration. But the person in whose soul the eternal is implanted seeks and aspires. If the visible does not deceive him, as the person is deceived who grasps the shadow instead of the form, if temporality does not deceive him, as the person is deceived who is continually waiting for tomorrow, if the temporary does not deceive him, as the person is deceived who procrastinates along the way — if this does not happen, then the world does not quiet his longing. Then it helps him only by means of repulsion to seek further, to seek the eternal, God's kingdom, which is above in the heavens — as high as this bird has never gone; the bird that flies the highest of all still flies beneath the heavens. Seek first God's kingdom — *'which is within you.'*" (*Edifying Discourses in Various Spirits*) ■

Above: Esrom Monastery which Kierkegaard would have passed on his way to Gilleleje.
Below: Kierkegaard's favorite spot at Gilbjerg outside Gilleleje. The inscription on the rock reads, "What is truth other than to fully live for an idea?"

I realize more and more that I am so constituted that I shall not succeed in realizing my ideals, while in another sense . . . I shall grow far beyond my ideals. Ordinarily, most people aim their ideals at the Great, the Extraordinary, which they never attain. I am far too melancholy to harbor such ideals. Others would smile at my ideals. It is certainly true that my ideal was simply to become a husband, to live solely for being married. And lo and behold, while I despair of attaining that goal I become an author and, who knows, maybe a ranking author. My next ideal was to become a minister in a rural parish and live amid quiet scenery, become an integral part of the small circle surrounding me – and lo and behold, as I despair of attaining that, it is quite possible that I shall again realize something that will appear much greater. Journals 1846

*N*o sooner have I taken pen in hand, when at that very instant I am incapable of moving it. . . . It seems to me as if I hear a voice saying to me: "Silly fellow, what does he imagine? Does he not know that obedience is dearer to God than the fat of rams?" Then I become perfectly quiet, then there is time enough to painfully write each letter with my slow pen. And if that poetic impatience awakens in me again for an instant, it seems as though I hear a voice speaking to me as a teacher speaks to a boy when he says, "Now hold the pen right, and form each letter with equal precision." And then I can do it, then I dare not do otherwise, then I write every word, every line, almost without knowing what the next word or the next line will be. And afterwards when I read it over it satisfies me in quite a different way. (For though it may be that one or another glowing expression escapes me, yet the production is quite a different one: it is the outcome, not of the poet or the thinker's passion, but of godly fear, and for me it is a form of divine worship. (From The Point of View for My Work as an Author)

3
AUTHOR

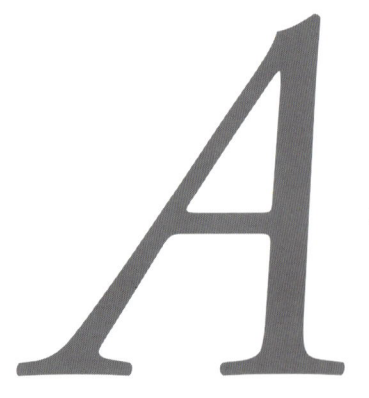

Although Kierkegaard experienced a spiritual revival around the time of his father's death, he had still only gained entry to the initial courtyard of the Holy of Holies of the Christian faith. It was within this seeming void that he began his career as author. From 1841, when he returned from Berlin, until 1846, he wrote the bulk of his literary works, several of which would never have been written in the form they were, had there been no unhappy romance with Regine. Both *Either/Or, Fear and Trembling, Repetition,* and *Stages* were all written with her specifically in mind. They were his way of explaining his reasons for breaking with Regine. As a result, a deep analysis of the human condition developed. A philosophy gradually unfolded as thoughts poured out through Kierkegaard's facile pen in an uncontrolled torrent. In the years 1843-1844 alone, Kierkegaard published twelve books: six literary works with his "left hand" (under different pseudonyms) and six religious "speeches" (as he humbly called them) with his "right." At the same time he continued faithfully confiding in his journals, which are an indispensable contribution toward understanding his works, and by means of which any Kierkegaard student can get a sense of reading over the shoulder of a complex writer even as his philosophy is taking shape. This is because the journals "confront us with the thinker as he existed, and etch a life in glimpses which, though fragmentary, constitute something else and more than a biography, in fact something unique in world literature," according to Peter Rohde (*The*

My becoming an author is due chiefly to her, my melancholy, and my money. Journals 1843

I save my life, or keep myself alive, by writing. Journals 1848

One thought chases the next; no sooner have I thought it and am about to write it down than a new one comes along - hold it, grasp it - Madness - Insanity! Journals 1837

Left: Dyrehaven north of Copenhagen. Right: Josty's Konditori in the Frederiksberg Gardens where Kierkegaard often went for a walk.

38

Diary of Søren Kierkegaard, Carol Publishing Group, New York, 1993). Alongside a hectic and successful career both as a philosophical, pseudonymous author and a radical, religious writer working under his own name, Kierkegaard also sustained a busy social life with "worldly pleasures" during most of the 1840s. He took frequent walks along the streets or on the ramparts around the city where he chatted with people or hoped to catch a glimpse of Regine. He often took carriage rides to his favorite spots in Dyrehaven and then ended the day with a lavish meal. Maybe he was trying to demonstrate with his irresponsible lifestyle that Regine was better off without him. He certainly felt unworthy of her love. Perhaps he wanted to publicly give the impression that he was good for nothing, a man whose books should not be judged according to the vices of their author but according to the virtues of their contents. In any case, Kierkegaard continued living a double life in which he spent the days enjoying the pleasures of the world and the nights after coming home from his escapades, writing passionately and reading religious books for the edification of his soul. He was tormented, a haunted spirit, caged like a bird that dies unless it keeps on singing, a sinner approaching God with "sympathetic antipathy and antipathetic sympathy." During the 1840s he wrote book after book with a nervous energy that helped him forget his unhappy fate and soothed his inner pain. "Of very few authors," says Lee M. Hollander in *Selections from the Writings of Kierkegaard*, "can it be said with the same literalness as of Kierkegaard that their life is their ministry; as if to furnish living proof of his untiring insistence on inwardness, his life, like that of so many other spiritual educators of the race, is notably poor in incidents; but his life of inward experiences is all the richer – witness the 'literature within the literature' that came to be within a few years and that gave to Danish letters a score of immortal works."

Finally in 1846 he paused, took another deep breath and wrote the *Postscript* with which he had planned to end his literary career and publicly explain the purpose behind his authorship. Then he would retire from his writing and become a minister in some country parish, he thought. But something happened that changed his plans and sent Kierkegaard back to his writing desk with renewed passion. ∎

Only when I write do I feel well. Then I forget all of life's vexations, all its sufferings, then I am wrapped in thought and am happy. . . . So powerful an urge, so ample, so inexhaustible, one which, having subsisted day after day for five or six years, is still flowing as richly as ever, such an urge, one would think, must also be a vocation from God. Journals 1847

Here was a religious author who began as an aesthetic author . . . but I totally lacked sincerity. The Point of View 1848

The author of Either/Or *devoted a definite time every day, regularly and with monastic precision, to reading for his own sake edifying books, and in fear and much trembling he reflected upon his responsibility.* The Point of View 1848

I have a thorn in the flesh since my earliest days. If it hadn't been for that, I should probably have progressed far in worldliness by now. But I cannot, no matter how much I might wish to. Journals 1848

It is now my idea to train myself for the ministry. These many months past I have prayed God to help me on my way, for it has long been clear to me that I ought not to continue as an author any longer; if I did I would want to be one completely, or not at all. Journals, February 7, 1846

The Master and the Secretary

The master's house stood in Nytorv, situated between a court building and a pharmacy. On one side people were healed for their sicknesses, on the other they were judged for their transgressions.

On the first floor lived the single individual who was sufficient to himself in a world where people only felt themselves whenever they gathered in crowds and imitated each other. . . .

This was the laboratory of thoughts, the birthplace of ideas.

On the sunlit marketplace below, the mob and their slaves bargained and bought. In the middle of the fountain sat Charitas with her two children, and above the red-tiled houses around the marketplace rose Our Lady's Church with its golden cross reminding the forgetful of the Christian faith.

The master was working, regular as a clock. Project after project flowed from his magic hands — great and bulky works on life, both the earthly as well as the heavenly. The lonely master had retired to the innermost cave of his mountain where he spun gold of thoughts on his spinning wheel of ideas, year after year. His apartment, full of books and writing materials, was closed to the public, and this meant more or less everyone. Only a little Jew, Israel Salomon Levin, was allowed in for free. He was the master's secretary, a sort of Famulus to the great Faust of Christianity. He was a small, dark man, extremely smart, and consistently cynical. He came and went like a serving spirit, and since he was a Jew, considered a neutral necessity in the household.

The master always wrote industriously, and every one of his works ended up being a masterpiece. . . .

The small nimble man looked up to his master, even though their religions were worlds apart. Levin enjoyed being in the crucible of the spirit. As soon as he walked through the sacrosanct doors, his dubious, dark eyes sparkled in malicious delight at the fact that he was the favorite. To this man, everything in these three magic rooms facing the street was significant. The writing desk was a marvelous piece of furniture where masterpieces of great depth were unceasingly turned out. This was the secretary, the place where books were drafted during the late, consecrated hours of the night. Then there were the bookshelves, the enviable places where all the Church fathers and philosophers of the world silently witnessed to the miraculous triumph of thoughts and words over sluggish matter. From these favored rooms the whole world was conquered. Here battles were fought, one after the other. Here the idea was fighting for its very survival. Here was the battleground of the spirits. ■

(Svend Leopold, *Søren Kierkegaard: Geniets tragedie*, Gyldendal, Copenhagen 1932)

Top: Købmagergade with the Round Tower in the background (end of the 19th century). Middle: Regensen and the Round Tower. Bottom: Students at Regensen, 1830.

Kierkegaard Around the World

Interview with Kinya Masugata

Kinya Masugata is professor of Ethics at Osaka Kyoiku University, Japan. He obtained his master's degree in ethics in 1976 and is a Ph.D. candidate. He is a member of both The Kansai Ethical Society and The Japanese Association of Philosophical and Ethical Research in Medicine. He has translated texts by Kierkegaard into Japanese and written numerous articles on the Danish philosopher. His favorite Kierkegaard quote is, "Possibility is the weightiest of all categories."

I understand that you became aquainted with Kierkegaard's philosophy many years ago by reading a Japanese edition translated from the German?
Yes, that was in my college days when a teacher introduced me to Kierkegaard's ideas. At that time, Kierkegaard was already extremely popular among intellectuals in my country, especially his books *The Sickness Unto Death* and *The Concept of Anxiety*. I first read *The Sickness Unto Death*, which by now has over fifty reprints in Japanese, and was immediately filled with both sympathy and antipathy — sympathy because of his deep analysis of the various stages of despair, and antipathy because I felt he exposed the darkness in myself. But I continued to come back and read. Eventually I became so fascinated by what I read that I wrote my master's thesis on the concept of possibility in Kierkegaard.

How in the world can a Christian philosopher like Kierkegaard, hardly understood in his own culture and language, end up halfway across the world and be understood in a culture totally different from his own?
Following the Meiji period which began in 1868, Japanese scholars were first introduced to European

> **I first read The Sickness Unto Death, and was immediately filled with both sympathy and antipathy — sympathy because of his deep analysis of the various stages of despair, and antipathy because I felt he exposed the darkness in myself.**

> *The reception of Kierkegaard in Japan reveals an understanding of Kierkegaard which is different than that of his countrymen and other Europeans. It not only presents a new way of understanding Kierkegaard, but also deepens our way of understanding ourselves.*

cultural traditions and Western styles of thinking. The philosophy teachers from the Kyoto school were especially influenced by Kierkegaard. The foremost philosopher in Japan, Nisida Kitaro, who is a Zen Buddhist, proposed his own way of thinking by using Kierkegaard's terms. Another postwar philosopher from the Kyoto school, Tanabe Hajime, wrote a great book about the philosophy of repentance (Metanoetic). This book was greatly influenced by Kierkegaard as well. And finally I should mention Nishitani Keiji who wrote a book entitled *What Is Religion?* He was also influenced by Kierkegaard. As you know, we have a long Buddhistic tradition in Japan, and before the Meiji era, Buddhistic thinking was traditional and less philosophical. In our transition from a traditional to a modern Buddhistic outlook, Kierkegaard's philosophy has been very helpful, especially his concept of appropriation (Danish "tilegnelse"). Until then we had no language that could adequately explain our Buddhistic experience in philosophical terms. Although Kierkegaard's terms were rooted in Christianity, we were able to convert them into the Japanese-Buddhistic experience. The meaning of the concepts may differ greatly between Christianity and Buddhism, but I suppose that the method is similar.

In other words, Kierkegaard has helped Japanese Buddhists become better Buddhists?

You could put it that way. For example, the idea of Amitaba in the Pureland sect of Japanese Buddhism has a similarity with the concept of God as a Person, but you have to remember that we understand ourselves through Kierkegaard's thinking, not Kierkegaard's thought itself. Nevertheless, I would like to mention that the reception of Kierkegaard in Japan reveals an understanding of Kierkegaard which is different than that of his countrymen and other Europeans. It not only presents a new way of understanding Kierkegaard, but also deepens our way of understanding ourselves. I hope that this different way of understanding Kierkegaard will be illuminating to other scholars as well.

And now you and a team of other translators are, for the first time in history, translating Kierkegaard from the original Danish into Japanese?

Yes. I have translated *Judge for Yourself!* and am now working on *The Concept of Anxiety*. Like many other scholars around the world, I have had to learn Danish because of Kierkegaard. But I don't speak it yet. Even though Danish is the hardest language to learn - next to Japanese, of course - I would like to have a chance to learn to speak Danish.

■

The Literary Works

Kierkegaard's works are not easy reading, especially the "left-handed," pseudononymous works in which he laid the groundwork for his religious writings. This article may serve as an overview of the works covering his first literary period, from 1841 (*The Concept of Irony*) to 1846 (*Concluding Unscientific Postscript*).

On the Concept of Irony, with Continual Reference to Socrates was Kierkegaard's magisterial dissertation, and although this book of 300 pages is not considered a major work, it is still extremely significant because it reveals his modus operandi, his method of and basic attitude about communicating as a philosopher. All his later works developed from the analysis of the "indirect method of communication" used by his great hero Socrates. Like Socrates, who questioned the universal assumptions and general knowledge of his day by way of a "midwifery" method that forced his listeners to look for the truth within themselves, so Kierkegaard wanted to demolish any philosophical system or theological belief that superimposed its values and norms on the individual. Only one's innermost self was to be the determining factor in the development of one's life. But unlike his hero, Kierkegaard did not believe that man has the divine truth within himself; it has come to him from outside himself, yet man has perverted the truth by taming it and laying claim to its promises without obeying its conditions.

Either/Or (1843), generally considered as Kierkegaard's first major work, has the outward appearance of a novel in which the ethical view of life comes face-to-face with the aesthetical. It begins with a series of aphorisms (diapsalmata) which help define the aesthetic life. This is followed by a number of essays which further illustrate the outcome of the aesthetic life, including an analysis of the psychology behind Mozart's *Don Juan*. This first part of *Either/Or* culminates in the "Diary of the Seducer," a partially autobiographical section based on Kierkegaard's own failed engagement to Regine.

The second part is an eloquent argument by "Judge William" in favor of the ethical, consciencious life with its sanctioned institutions and general law. This part seems less convincing, perhaps because at this point in his life Kierkegaard was already anticipating his "third stage," the religious life, where he would grapple with the question of how one becomes a Christian with heart and mind intact. This would become the theme of the rest of his works. The book concludes with a sermon, which serves as an introduction to this theme.

In *Fear and Trembling* (1843) and *Repetition* (1843) Kierkegaard discusses the nature of the ethical life and defines the religious sphere. *Fear and Trembling* is a brilliant study of how Abraham, the father of faith, transgresses general law with the religious act of obeying God's seemingly absurd command to kill his son Isaac. By doing this Abraham becomes "the exception," the brave individual who, in fear and trembling, supercedes the ethical law of society and gains back by faith that which he has risked. In *Repetition* Kierkegaard further illustrates this idea within the context of his own renunciation of Regine.

Philosophical Fragments (1844) expounds the nature of faith in relation to the paradox of God becoming man in Jesus Christ. The book is an objection to any system of thought attempting to limit the paradox of faith, and it is here that Kierkegaard first introduces the concept of "contemporaneousness" with Christ.

The Concept of Anxiety (1844), together with *The Sickness Unto Death*, is considered Kierkegaard's principal psychological work. In this splendid analysis of our sinful human condition, Kierkegaard talks about anxiety as "the dizziness of freedom" that constitutes our human potential and precedes the leap of faith.

Prefaces (1844) is a series of attacks on the German philosopher, Georg Hegel's idealism as it manifested itself in Denmark at the time.

Stages on Life's Way (1845) is an elaboration on the themes of *Either/Or* and *Repetition*. The first part, "In Vino Veritas" (The Banquet), is considered Kierkegaard's most outstanding literary work, surpassing even Plato's *Symposion*. The last part, "Guilty/Not Guilty," which Kierkegaard himself regarded as his best work, contains details concerning his own failed relationship with Regine.

Every one of the above-mentioned works was paving the way for Kierkegaard's attempt to answer a question which refused to let him go as he approached his religious breakthrough of 1848: How does one become a Christian? In his final literary work from this period, *Concluding Unscientific Postscript to the Philosophical Fragments* (1846), Kierkegaard once and for all establishes the subjectivity of faith, as opposed to the objectivity of assent: no system, no church, no dogma, not even unwavering faith in the biblical testimony, can take the place of the leap of saving, subjective faith by which the individual must daily attain Christianity. ■

I was seated as usual, out of doors at the cafe in the Frederiksberg Garden.... I had been a student for half a score of years. Although never lazy, all my activity nevertheless was like a glittering inactivity, a kind of occupation for which I still have a great partiality, and for which perhaps I even have a little genius....

So there I sat smoking my cigar until I lapsed into thought. Among other thoughts I remember these: "You are going on," I said to myself, "to become an old man, without being anything, and without really undertaking to do anything. On the other hand, wherever you look about you, in literature and in life, you see the celebrated names and figures, the precious and much heralded men who are coming into prominence and are much talked about, the many benefactors of the age who know how to benefit mankind by making life easier and easier, some by railroads, others by omnibuses and steamboats, others by the telegraph, others by easily apprehended compendiums and short recitals of everything worth knowing, and finally the true benefactors of the age who make spiritual existence and virtue of thought easier and easier, yet more and more significant. And what are you doing?" Here my soliloquy was interrupted, for my cigar was smoked out and a new one had to be lit. So I smoked again, and then suddenly this thought flashed through my mind: "You must do something, but inasmuch as with your limited capacities it will be impossible to make anything easier than it has become, you must, with the same humanitarian enthusiasm as the others, undertake to make something harder." This notion pleased me immensely, and at the same time it flattered me to think that I, like the rest of them, would be loved and esteemed by the whole community. For when all combine in every way to make everything easier, there remains only one possible danger, namely, that the ease becomes so great that it becomes altogether too great; then there is only one want left, though it is not yet a felt want, when people will want difficulty. Out of love for mankind, and out of despair at my embarrassing situation, seeing that I had accomplished nothing and was unable to make anything easier than it had already been, and moved by a genuine interest in those who make everything easy, I conceived it my task to create difficulties everywhere.

Postscript 1846

44

4
PHILOSOPHER

Back in the summer of 1835, Kierkegaard vacationed in the fishing village of Gilleleje about forty miles north of Copenhagen. It was here that he first caught a glimpse of a vision that would carry him beyond the nonchalance of an arrogant youth into the manhood of a responsible, religious individual. At his favorite spot on the cliffs of Gilbjerg he feverishly filled his journal with ideas and insights which would become the starting point of a philosophy intertwined with his own spiritual development. But, as we have seen, his father's "sickness unto death" set him back and threw him headlong into doubt, self-indulgence and despair. From 1835 to 1841 Kierkegaard rebelled against a bourgeois version of a Christianity which he considered sick and effete, but he was unable to find anything to replace it. In *The Sickness Unto Death*, he later provided a compelling illustration of his own spiritual state during those years: "A self which desperately wants to be itself moans from agony which will not go away or part from his concrete self. Precisely on this pain he throws all his passion until it turns into demonic rage. Even if God in heaven with all His angels would offer to help him, he is no longer willing to be helped, it is too late . . . he would rather be outraged at everything, be the ultimate wronged person in all the world. In his rage against existence the desperate one thinks he has found a proof against all goodness. He himself is the proof, this is what he wants to be. Therefore he wants to be himself, himself in his agony, because in this agony he will protest against existence."

As he effectively burned his bridges behind him, Kierkegaard slowly began to discover a new landscape of virtue and ethical faith. But before he could enter the land of hope and personal faith he was again dragged back through the mud of repentance and despair. "The whole of existence frightens me," he wrote in 1839, "from the smallest fly to the mystery of the incarnation; everything is unintelligible to me, most of all myself; the whole of existence is poisoned in my sight, particularly myself. Great is my sorrow and without bounds; no man knows it, only God in heaven and He will not console me. . . . Young man, you who still stand at the beginning of the way, if you have gone astray, O be converted, turn to God and be taught by Him so your youth will be strengthened to the work of manhood; you will never experience what he must suffer who, after having vasted the strength and courage of his youth in rebellion against Him, must now, exhausted and powerless, begin a retreat through desolate and devastated provinces surrounded on all sides by the

---

I shall now try to fix a calm gaze upon myself and begin to act in earnest; for only thus shall I be able, like the child calling itself 'I' with its first conscious action, to call myself "I" in any deeper sense.
Journals, August 1, 1835

Conversion goes slowly. As Franz Baader rightly observes, one has to walk back by the same road he came out on earlier. It is easy to become impatient; if it cannot happen at once, one may just as well let it go, begin tomorrow, and enjoy today; this is the temptation. Is that not the meaning of the words: to take God's kingdom by force? This is why we are told to work out our salvation in fear and trembling, for it is not finished or completed; backsliding is a possibility.
Journals, July 3, 1836

abomination of desolation, by burnt towns and the delusive expectations of smoking sites, by trampled down prosperity and broken strength, a retreat as slow as a bad year, as long as eternity monotonously broken by the sound of the complaint: these days please me not." *(Journals, May 12, 1839)*

It was in this landscape of repentance and return to the truth of Christianity that Kierkegaard's philosophy was to develop, a philosophy that would "rouse his contemporaries from their philosophic complacency and unwarrented optimism and move them to realize that the spiritual life has both mountain and valley, that it is no flat plain easy to travel," according to Lee M. Hollander. After his years of skepticism, he came to believe in an objective Truth, not inaccessible to us but made accessible in the "direct speech" of Christianity. And since Christianity is Truth present in existence, we can only know it to be true by relating ourselves to it subjectively, in existence. Kierkegaard soon realized that, contrary to his father's inward and intense Christian faith, the common version of the Faith as it was preached and practiced within the Danish State Church system, was far from the standard of New Testament Christianity. In this gap between the ideal and the actual he found the idea for which he could live and die. He devoted himself to the *dialectics of subjectivity*, defying any system or convenient approach that would *explain* reality and make life manageable. For this purpose he successfully put to work the dialectical method in which he had been tutored by his father whenever Michael had demolished his opponents' arguments by means of his superior analytical mind. As Kenneth Hamilton said, "We continue to listen to Kierkegaard, not because he provides us with an intriguing case history of a morbid personality, but because he seems to have something to say to us that we do not find elsewhere. Moreover, he shames us whenever we feel inclined to reject his conclusions out of hand, by flashing before us a rigor of mind that shows up the flabbiness of our customary ways of thinking. He decidely will not be patronized. And, when we are inclined to excuse ourselves by saying that this is all intellectual legerdemain, and that there is a big flaw somewhere that vitiates his whole argument, then he challenges us to put our finger on the precise place where he goes wrong. And this is not so easy, because, if we find one spot where we think we can wriggle out of his logic, then he has twenty other propositions ready, waiting for us and asking us if we really wish to test our skill against his." (*The Promise of Kierkegaard*, Lippincott, New York, 1969, pgs. 24-25)

Kierkegaard certainly possessed a rare ability to define a thought, to trace its implications and consequences, and to juxtapose it against differing views. His mission, however, is not to debate on a philosophical basis for the sake of winning an argument. He challenges us to share a vision of life, to dare subjectivity as an appropriation of objective truth for the sake of personal action. For Kierkegaard, a bullet-

I mean to labor to achieve a far more inward relation to Christianity; hitherto I have fought for its truth while in a sense standing outside it. In a purely outward sense I have carried Christ's cross, like Simon of Cyrene.
Journals, July 9, 1838

All other religions are oblique. The founder stands aside and introduces another speaker, they themselves therefore come under religion - Christianity alone is direct speech (I am the truth).
Journals 1837

Every truth is nevertheless truth only to a certain degree; when it goes beyond, the counterpoint appears and it becomes untruth. Journals

If I am capable of grasping God objectively, I do not believe, but precisely because I cannot do this I must believe. The Postscript

proof argument is no guarantee that truth has been arrived at anyway. Truth only happens by relating oneself to the Truth. Truth only gives meaning in relation to the life of the individual; it cannot be isolated to a method of rational speculation. This does not mean that just any kind of subjectivity is acceptable. The widespread idea of individualism as self-assertion, as a principle of If-it-feels-right-to-me-then-it's-true-for-me, is left over from Romanticism and is as foreign to Kierkegaard as can be. What he said was that ultimate Truth, Christianity, is available to any individual through a choice, a leap of faith beyond reason, never to the many inside Christendom who ironically reject the radical claims of Christianity by making it a comfortable and reasonable lifestyle. Kierkegaard was no system-builder, and therefore he was not interested in reforming Christendom within the prison of enlightenment and doctrinal assent. He preferred to see himself, not as a reformer that was to change Christendom, but as a prosecutor who would expose its fallacies by holding up the New Testament ideal and arousing the individual to a desperate awareness and radical choice.

Christianity is not a doctrine but an existential communication expressing an existential contradiction. The Postscript

Kierkegaard spelled out his philosophy in terms such as *Anxiety, Despair, Paradox of faith, the Moment, the Choice, Possibility, Repetition, Reduplication, Transition,* and *Transformation* — all essential concepts in Kierkegaard's works. It goes beyond the purpose of this book to explain the complex reality of these themes. However, in order to understand the primary principle running through Kierkegaard's literary studies and implied in his religious discourses, it would be helpful to outline the three general stages, or modes of living, which he introduced in his first important book, *Either/Or* (partly written in Berlin in 1841), and later enunciated and further analyzed in his final aesthetic works, the *Stages* (1845) and the *Postscript* (1846). Kierkegaard based his starting point on Hegel's three evolutionary *stages* of consciousness in the development of mankind: 1. a primitive consciousness at the level of sense experience; 2. moral consciousness as an appreciation of law and reason; 3. self-consciousness rising to awareness of one's own nature. Kierkegaard changed Hegel's three successive stages to three overlapping *spheres* of existence among people outside the Christian faith. Only by maturing beyond each stage and moving forward into the next through the moment of responsible choice, can a human being arrive at the paradox of Christian faith and follow Christ in total submission to God. To be a Christian, then, means to become *contemporaneous* with Christ, to live in a relationship with Him in the same intense way the first disciples did, suffering the paradox of faith and the rejection of the crowd.

Christianity is very far behind. One must begin with paganism. And so I begin with Either/Or. Journals

The first sphere is the *aesthetic* view of life, a life of immediacy determined by externals, an attitude of self-indulgence for the sake of satisfying one's basic desires. Kierkegaard had personally lived this lifestyle through to its bitter end, and his verdict is that it leads to a dissolution of the self and finally to boredom or despair; life simply falls apart into disconnected moods and random impulses. One of the very first entries in his journals reads, "I have just returned from a party of which I was the life and soul; witty banter flowed from my lips, everyone laughed and admired me – but I came away, indeed that dash should be as long as the radii of the earth's orbit——————————— wanting to shoot myself." If the aesthetic person admits his despair to himself and wants to change, the only way out is to choose one's self by means of a free, responsible act.

The next sphere is the *ethical* lifestyle. The person who has chosen himself through repentance will no longer live for himself within a split self. Kierkegaard's ethical pseudonym Judge William sums it up like this, "Not until a person in his choice has taken himself upon himself, has put on himself, has totally interpenetrated himself so that every movement he makes is accompanied by a consciousness of responsibility for himself - not until then has a person chosen himself ethically, not until then is he concrete, not until then is he in his total isolation in absolute continuity with the actuality to which he belongs." (*Either/Or*) The ethical lifestyle, however, eventually leads to a crisis since it does not satisfy the basic need of the spirit within which is eternal.

Only through a leap of faith can the ethical person reach the third sphere, the *religious* lifestyle, which is characterized by faith in the eternal from which the human spirit springs. Kierkegaard distinguishes between two forms of religious orientation: a Religion A (a general religious philosophy of life where the eternal nullifies time, as in most religions) and a Religion B (the paradox of the Christian faith where the eternal enters time through the incarnation of God in Christ). True Christianity is trust in the paradox of the incarnation and a contemporaneous life with Christ.

Kierkegaard's basic philosophy, which developed with an amazing consistency in the course of writing his books, was that life consists of a series of passages, or crises, through which a person will either lose himself and become increasingly demonized or will gain himself by becoming spirit. The most severe crisis *in extremis* a person may face is the crisis of faith which occurs when he takes hold of the paradox and dives into the "70,000 fathoms" of God's grace in order to receive full forgiveness of sins. "Believing that his sins have been forgiven," Kierkegaard wrote in his journal, "is the decisive crisis through which a human being becomes spirit. He who does not believe that is not spirit. It constitutes spiritual maturity; it means that all spontaneity has been lost, that man not only cannot do anything of himself, but can only do harm to himself. But how many experience in actual truth, quite personally, the understanding of themselves that they have been brought to such an extremity? (Herein lies the Absurd, the scandal, the paradox, the forgiveness of sins.)"

The year he wrote this was 1848, the year that would come to mark his own personal homecoming and leap of faith into the paradoxical grace of God. Up until then he had been writing with increasing passion *about* being a Christian. Now was the time to act by *becoming* one himself. ■

I have looked in vain for an anchorage in the boundless sea of pleasure and in the depth of understanding; I have felt the almost irresistible power with which one pleasure reaches out its hand to the next. . . . It seems as though I had not drunk from the cup of wisdom, but had fallen into it. Journals 1835

There lies the problem of my own life. A very old man raised me in extremely strict Christianity, and that is why I feel my life to be so terribly confused. . . . Not until now, in my thirty-fifth year, have I learned – by dint of heavy suffering and with the bitterness of repentance – to die to the world to the extent that I might truly find my life and my salvation in a belief centering on the forgiveness of sin. . . . He who then in truth has experienced, and experiences, the belief that his sins have been forgiven probably becomes a changed man. . . . This man has added an eternity to his age; for now that he has become spirit, all spontaneity and attendant selfishness, his selfish clinging to the world and to his own self, are lost. Now, humanly speaking, he is old, extremely old, but from the viewpoint of eternity he is young. Journals 1848

A Philosophy of Hope

Interview with Howard Hong

> *For Kierkegaard, individualism then means to become genuinely human, a responsible individual, the universal singular, yet to remain distinct from the crowd, because those in the undifferentiated public are anonymous.*

Professor Howard Hong is a lifelong student of Kierkegaard. Since 1939 when he and Edna H. Hong first translated Kierkegaard's *For Self-examination*, they have translated most of Kierkegaard's papers into English. They presently are working on a new translation of Kierkegaard's book on Adler, due to be completed in 1997.

Kierkegaard is considered a philosopher of individualism. Explain what that means.
Let me first say what it does not mean. It is not a form of romantic individualism, not rootless, arbitrary individualism. For Kierkegaard the individual is a representative of the universal and essential, but the individual should become an *authentic* individual. That's why in the new translation, preference is given to the term *the single individual*. *Single* means integral. And *single individual* means the universal singular, not merely a specimen of a type, but someone with authenticity because the choice has been made to become integrated in one's understanding. Spirit is the power one's understanding exercises over one's life. One has taken responsibility for one's life in the context of the universally human. There is not only a phenomenology in Kierkegaard, but an ontology and a philosophical anthropolog, as well.

How does Kierkegaard's concept of the individual differ from our modern understanding of individualism?
The basis for modern individualism, as we have it from Sartre for example, is that there is no universal human nature or essence. For Kierkegaard there is a human nature. For Kierkegaard, individualism then means to become genuinely human, a responsible individual, the universal singular, yet to remain distinct from the crowd, because those in the undifferentiated public are anonymous. There is nobody there, no one is responsible. That's why Kierkegaard wrote so much against the public, the mob, *the idolatry of the masses*, where there is no individual responsibility. According to Kierkegaard, this also

meant something we need very much today: a concern and respect for our neighbor, the person next to us, the people we meet.

Why then, is Kierkegaard being read more today than ever before?
Kierkegaard had something to say about this. "Not much attention is paid to what I have to say," he wrote, "although there are those who like what I have offered with my left hand. But the day will come when things will get so desperate that there will be need for people like me." That's what I think has happened. We have been on a real decline in many ways. We talk about progress, self-esteem, human rights, of being human, and so on, because we suspect that we don't have these things. That's why we talk about them so much. When I was growing up, we didn't talk about these things; we assumed them. Kierkegaard was correct that we live in desperate times, because we live in an empirical world of physics, chemistry, biology, and empirical psychology, sciences descriptive of what is. We live in an age of *isms* and dehumanization, a decadent age that is more brutal, more violent, more bloody, more contentious than ever before.

Abortion is a prime example of this. All this is romantic, arbitrary individualism. The mother doesn't die for her child; she kills her child. We now realize that we do not have a radical concept of what it is to be a self, and in Kierkegaard one can find what it means to be a self. In the opening chapter of *The Sickness Unto Death*, for instance, there are one-and-a-half compact pages containing much of the essence of what Kierkegaard has to say about what it is to be human (see Reader). One may not understand it at first, but then one should read it again and again until one does understand. This is self-knowledge, not massaging flattery and petty talk about self-esteem, but self-knowledge to the point of despair and a new vision of possibility.

So self-knowledge is not progress but regression?
Yes, spiritual progress means going backward and downward or deeper. Self-knowledge, in relation to the highest ideal, does not produce self-esteem. It's the opposite, you see. This is why even in *Either/Or*, Judge William says to the young man, "You are in despair. What you should do, then, is to despair as a conscious act. And in doing that, you will gain

> *We talk about progress, self-esteem, human rights, of being human, and so on, because we suspect that we don't have these things. That's why we talk about them so much.*

> A conscious act means to take responsibility for oneself. In this act one is on the way to being healed of despair, because one sees oneself transparently and can accept the gift of resting in the power that established it, in other words, one receives forgiveness.

yourself." A conscious act means to take responsibility for oneself. In this act one is on the way to being healed of despair, because one sees oneself transparently ("gennemsigtigt," in the Danish, a big word for Kierkegaard) and can accept the gift of resting in the power that established it; in other words, one receives forgiveness. Kierkegaard sums it up in his *Journals and Papers*: "What is the Christian life?" he asks and gives this answer: "It is essentially grace." But it is not grace taken in vain, because it actually takes grace to accept grace. And in gratitude there is born a new responsive, indicative ethics and a motivation for continuing to strive.

Despair *is a complicated word for Kierkegaard - as is* doubt. *Do we have to doubt in order to believe?*
Despair is an intensification of doubt to the point where there is no more hope. Doubt ("tvivl" in the Danish) means *dual,* and Kierkegaard's term for despair ("fortvivlelse" in the Danish) means *to be dual,* to have a divided self to the point of no other possibility. The self is not integrated. That's why we prefer to use the term "the *single* individual" for the authentic self that relates to itself by having chosen itself in a conscious act of reflection, freedom, and choice. In becoming itself, the self is no longer split, but integrated in a vision of the essentially human. There is a human nature, but the individual is born *potentially* human; it still needs to *become* authentically human, and it is in that becoming that the self proves its humanness. Ultimately it can only do this by resting in the gift of grace and forgiveness, in which there is hope beyond hopelessness, possibility beyond impossibility.

But despair points back to another condition that is essential for Kierkegaard. He calls this condition *anxiety* ("angst" in the Danish). We all have a sense of anxiety, an ambiguous restlessness that has no object as fear does. Only human beings know anxiety as a *dizziness of freedom,* an ambiguous frustration of not being able to realize our freedom. Doubt is the state between anxiety and despair. Doubt is thought's despair; despair is the self's radical doubt.

In Either/Or *Kierkegaard has described the stages, or spheres, of anxiety that lead to despair and finally to grace. Could you explain these stages?*
The first stage is the immediate, the immediate or spontaneous level where life is simply a satisfaction of desire. Kierkegaard calls this the *aesthetic* life. The problem with this way of life is that one is repeatedly frustrated because

one is never continually satisfied. Or, *if* one is satisfied, one becomes bored.

Second, there is the life of task. There is an ought. This is the *ethical* stage where there is an ideal of the highest good and a vision of life according to which the ethical person must live. Whereas the aesthetic is that whereby one is what one immediately is, the ethical is that whereby one becomes what one teleologically becomes what one becomes.

Third, there is a stage which Kierkegaard develops further in his *Postscript*. This is the *religious* stage. Religion A includes every view that has a sense of the eternal, that time is not all there is. Every religious form that strives to break through time into the eternal belongs under A. Religion B, on the other hand, which Kierkegaard considered identical with Christianity, means accepting the paradox that eternity has broken into time. It doesn't mean the abandonment of time as Plato and the Eastern religions require. It is far from abandonment of time. It is the *fulfillment* of time.

Which leads to some other big words for Kierkegaard, such as incarnation *and* revelation.
Yes, God became God in time through a teacher. In his *Philosophical Fragments* Kierkegaard has a wonderful parable about a king who wants to marry a peasant girl. If he marries her in his glory, it will crush her because she will always be conscious of the distance between them. So how can he win her without crushing her? He comes as a servant to her where she is; he lowers himself to her level, in this way winning her heart in freedom. This is the paradox of God in time, a descent in order to elevate.

What is your favorite Kierkegaard quote?
It's from the *Journals and Papers*. I can't give it to you accurately, but the substance, which we have already touched on, is: What is the Christian life? It is a vision of life, infinite humiliation in self-knowledge, the boundless grace of God, and a striving born of gratitude. Here you have all the elements of the stages on life's road, including the transformation of the imperative ethics into the responsive, indicative ethics. Another great line that encapsulates everything from another angle is in *The Sickness Unto Death,* where Kierkegaard says, "There is no immediate health of the spirit." This has to do with human nature, with anxiety and despair, which we don't like, but nevertheless are signs of the potential greatness of every human being. This is what it is to be human in the context of a philosophy of the future that redeems the past, a philosophy of possibility where there is no human possibility, a philosophy of hope in the midst of despair. ∎

> *What is the Christian life? It is a vision of life, infinite humiliation in self-knowledge, the boundless grace of God, and a striving born of gratitude. Here you have all the elements of the stages on life's road, including the transformation of the imperative ethics into the responsive, indicative ethics.*

53

Each person takes his revenge on the world. Mine consists in carrying my grief and anguish deeply embedded within myself, while my laughter entertains all. If I see somebody suffer I sympathize with him, console him to the best of my ability, and listen to him quietly when he assures me that I am fortunate. If I can keep this up to the day of my death I shall have had my revenge.   Journals 1837

When God wishes to bind a human being to Him in earnest, He summons one of His most faithful servants, His trustiest messenger, Grief, and tells him: "Hurry after him, overtake him, do not budge from his side. . . ." No woman clings more tenderly to what she loves than Grief.

Journals 1841

5
WITNESS

A particular incident helped Kierkegaard take the final step across the line between observance and profession, between just talking about Christianity and actually acting upon the radical claims he had himself so profoundly expounded. In 1846, *The Corsair*, a popular, satirical paper in Copenhagen, published a series of articles and cartoons in which Kierkegaard was made fun of. The articles were in response to Kierkegaard's contempt for *The Corsair's* style of journalism — its pandering to the lowest instincts of the mob and its assumption that people could not think for themselves. At first, Kierkegaard was shocked and deeply hurt by the articles and cartoons, but he decided to ignore his persecutors. The attack did however, make him feel ostracized and homeless in his own city, and he toyed with the idea of giving up his writing career and devoting himself to the salvation of his soul within the walls of some country parsonage. But that would have been running away from persecution. He chose to stay in the petty world of the Philistines which he predicted would become increasingly affected by popular democratic ideals, thanks to the press, which he called "the evil principle in our modern world." Through a series of bitter reflections on the Present Times he made a definitive break with the world and instead, chose the arena of martyrdom, joining the blood witnesses of old. Until now he had lived and fought for an idea. Now the time had come to die for it, just like the martyrs who had given their lives for the sake of the Gospel, in order to overthrow a heathen world. His task however, was not to overthrow heathens, but rather, to attack the caricature of Christianity which official Christendom had raised as its standard; to expose the blasphemy of the clergy who made Christianity seem permissive and secure instead of preaching and showing how difficult and

What is it to be roasted alive at a slow fire. . . in comparison with this torture: to be grinned to death! Journals 1846

God be praised that I was subjected to the attack of the rabble. I have now had time to arrive at the conviction that it was a melancholy thought to want to live in a vicarage, doing penance in an out-of-the-way place. Journals, January 24, 1847

For six months The Corsair *singled out Kierkegaard and exposed him to public ridicule by pointing at his uneven trouser legs and his ever-present umbrella, his lifestyle, and his broken relationship with Regine. Left: The local philosopher is pictured as the center of the universe. Right: Cartoon showing the anonymous author mustering his*

uncompromising it really is. Looking back on the incident a few years later, he wrote, "How important it has been. How this has taught me to understand myself, and to learn to know 'the world' and understand Christianity. Had this not happened, I probably would have missed out on something significant and lost the opportunity to get into a true relationship in the Christian faith." *(Journals 1850)* A splendid spiritual work from that time, *Upbuilding Discourses in Various Spirits* (1847), contains three of his most passionate and poetical discourses on the joys and the sufferings of the Christian life ("Purity of heart is to will one thing," "What we may learn from the lilies of the field and the birds of the air," and "The gospel of sufferings"). Kierkegaard dedicated the book to "the single individual," not least himself who in his own life had been so uncommitted. Here he showed that the narrow way to salvation must be traveled alone, as an individual, and that the world must be overthrown through persecution and death. The last part about suffering was the first of his many published discourses which he dared to call "Christian." In a follow-up, *Works of Love* (1847), Kierkegaard discussed the "how" of overcoming the world. *The Sickness Unto Death (*1849), *Practice in Christianity* (1850) and *For Self-Examination* (1851) followed in rapid succession, three more credits to Kierkegaard's religious authorship. The books were manifestos of undiluted Christianity and an indirectly scathing critique of the establishment, a compromising Church headed by Bishop Mynster of Copenhagen. Kierkegaard had reached another pinnacle in his authorship, he had written his final postscript and his point of view. From 1842 to 1851 he had written about thirty books and a twenty-volume journal, in "a single movement, in one breath." Now it was time to wait and see how Bishop Mynster and the Church would react to his ultimatum. Kierkegaard hoped for an admission: that Bishop Mynster would admit that the official Church was far from representing the kind of Christianity it professed.

All this time Kierkegaard had been struggling to become what he preached. Out of his inner work grew a sonorous confession of faith to the atoning sacrifice of Christ on the cross. Then finally, on April 19, 1848, for a moment the grace of God set his tormented heart free from the curse of guilt he had carried so long. "Now I believe in the forgiveness of sins," he wrote a few days later, "although I must carry my punishment for the rest of my life in this prison of reticence far from fellowship with other people. But I am pleased with the thought that God has forgiven me even

Left: Bishop Mynster's statue outside Our Lady's cathedral. Below: Our Lady's Cathedral with Thorvaldsen's famous statue of Christ. The statue inspired Kierkegaard to write a sermon which he later preached.

In the morning I get up and begin to thank God, then I set to work. At a certain time by night I quit, give thanks again and go to sleep. This is the way I live, although at certain moments I am overwhelmed by melancholy and sadness; but mostly I am living in a blessed enchantment day by day. Journals 1848

My whole nature is changed. My concealment and reserve are broken – I am free to speak!
Journals, April 19, 1848

No, no, my reserve still cannot be broken, at least not now.
Journals, April 24, 1848

though I am not so far as to say that this faith has erased my painful memories. However, as a believer I have protection against despair and bear the pain and punishment of reticence. I feel happy and blessed in the work of the Spirit which God has so graciously granted me." (*Journals, April 24, 1848*) The journal entries of April and May sing with joy and gratitude for the fact that God's grace is greater than the memory of sin and despair.

But Kierkegaard did not rest on the laurels of what happened in 1848. Throughout the seven years he still had left in life, he never once professed he was a Christian; he preferred to say that he was *becoming* one. Shortly before his death he made the radical claim that "when a person is truly serious about the fact that *he* is becoming a Christian, and that this is his task for the rest of his life, that all his efforts helping others to become Christians are only determining his own becoming a Christian - only then can a person relate to the infinite. As soon as he thinks, 'Now I am a Christian and I must make other people Christians too,' then Christianity is in reality lost." (*Journals 1855*)

Three years went by during which Kierkegaard worked diligently on his own becoming a Christian, a disciple of Christ. He had said what needed to be said and was waiting for Bishop Mynster's concession. But the bishop ignored him because he found him sacrilegous and wanted to avoid confrontation; the mob ridiculed Kierkegaard, and practically no one read his books (the *Concluding Postscript* had sold only sixty copies).

Then Bishop Mynster died in January, 1854. Professor Martensen, his successor, spoke at the funeral in Our Lady's cathedral. In his speech, Martensen praised Bishop Mynster as belonging to the long line of venerable witnesses to the truth. Martensen hereby gave the official, watered-down version of Christianity, which Mynster and the State Church represented, the seal of approval of true Christianity. This was too much for Kierkegaard. After Martensen's installment, Kierkegaard wrote a series of twenty-one polemic articles in the newspaper *Fædrelandet* and nine pamphlets in *The Moment* series where he claimed that "New Testament Christianity does not exist." Except for one vicious outburst in *Fædrelandet*, which only served to prove Bishop Martensen's inability to understand his opponent's purpose, the new bishop remained silent, and Kierkegaard took his case against Christendom into the streets. He was like a prophet pronouncing a desperate "midnight cry" of warning against the Church and its clergy.

On October 2, 1855, Kierkegaard was stricken down with paralysis on the street. He was taken to Frederiksberg Hospital, where he refused to receive Holy Communion from a member of the clergy. When asked by his lifelong friend, Emil Boesen, whether he believed in the grace of God in Christ, Kierkegaard replied, "Yes,

---

A hope was awakened in my soul that God may desire to resolve the fundamental misery of my being. That is to say, now I am in faith in the profoundest sense. Faith is the immediacy after reflection.
Journals 1848

Not even now will I call myself a Christian, no, I am still far behind.
The Moment 1855

Whatever I have accomplished, it does not interest me. The only thing that interests me is that I, by acting, have redeemed my eternal responsibility. God be praised, I have done it.
Journals, May 6, 1855

Christianly the emphasis does not fall so much upon what extent or how far a person succeeds in meeting or fulfilling the requirement, if he actually is striving, as it is upon his getting an impression of the requirement in all its infinitude so that he rightly learns to be humbled and to rely upon grace.
Journals 1851

of course, what else?" He died peacefully on November 11, 1855. His own prophetic words at the ending of *The Point of View* (1848) best encapsulate Kierkegaard's remarkable life and ministry: "He served the case of Christianity, his whole life, from childhood on, having been a wonderful preparation for just that task. He had completed the work of reflection, which was to place Christianity, what it means to be a Christian, totally within the act of reflection. Through his purity of heart he willed one thing only. But that which his contemporaries accused him of during his life, a stubborn refusal to compromise, became the very quality for which posterity would later praise him. He was not deceived by the great task before him. Whereas from a dialectical point of view, as an author he maintained an overview of the whole picture, from a religious standpoint he realized that it all served to urge him onward in his own personal education in Christianity. He had erected a dialectical structure using each of his works as building blocks, yet he was unable to dedicate this to any human being, much less himself. If it could have been dedicated to anyone, this would have been God, to whom the author had faithfully dedicated it day by day and year by year. According to the history books, the author was struck down by a deadly disease, but the poets say he died from longing for eternity so he finally would have nothing else to do but praise God."

God forbid that I claim my life resembles the life of Christ; may it only not be a satire of Him. How could I expect to be honored for speaking the truth – when He who was Truth was crucified? Journals 1848

Assistents Cemetery in Copenhagen where Kierkegaard is buried.

59

A Martyr of Laughter

A vegetable of a human being was walking the streets of the city, looking like no one else. His body was thin and fragile, and his eyes had a strangely frenzied, almost luminous shine to them. He always walked alone, carrying his large umbrella under his arm, which by now had become an object of public scorn. Sales clerks and shoemaker apprentices called him names. Those with nothing to do made loud comments about his odd outfits. What a spectacle!

But the work, the great work to which he had devoted his life, was finished. Following a life of suffering and struggle, this man had finally set the Christian standard before the eyes of mankind. The lonely man felt victorious, but the victory had ultimately exacted a price: a crown of thorns from his mockers was his only trophy. And so he smiled softly, and his mysterious eyes glistened with a light from beyond the beginning of time.

He had finally ended up in the shadow of his cross. And a miracle had happened. The distant Eternal One had come close and it was no longer possible to distinguish between the face of God and the face of Fate.

His feeble, nearly transparent body moved forward on the sidewalk, he looked as though a mere gust of wind could knock him over. The town was as it had always been, nothing could change its habits and outward appearance. Grocers would always be grocers, barbers would be barbers. The faces of fate were visible enough on families and individuals, but people had erected plates of colored glass between themselves and their daily routines, as a convenient way of adding color to their lives. They visited Tivoli amusement park, or the park. But the Great Countenance, that which was distant and inscrutable and painted into the death-marked master's face, was only seen in passing on Sundays between 10 and 11 a.m. For the rest of the week the public remained unmoved by the divine incarnation within him.

Life took its course.

Then it so happened that the bishop of Sjælland died. All the church bells rang, the journalists wrote orbituaries. The bishop had been a wise and sober-minded man, a good human intermediary between heaven and earth. As such, he had enjoyed good days in this life, and it was assumed he would enjoy good days in the next. He had made some enemies though, which is not uncommon among truly good people, but during his later years he had forgiven them all. Some people thought that he had weakly catered to a purely calculated and convenient philosophy of life, a cowardly consideration of earthly compromises. On the other hand, his supporters thought his white hair was venerable, for the years had earned him respect and importance. To many people he was a man of peace, a witness for Him who is beyond this world.

But now he was dead and the new bishop was Hans Lassen Martensen, a great scholar concerning the simple message of the Bible. Martensen said a few words in honor of the dead bishop, during which he allowed the countenance of the Eternal One to shine a little too brightly through his dead colleague's earthly existence. After all, he had managed to turn his life into quite a career. . . .

The new bishop claimed in front of the congregation that the former bishop had been a witness of truth, a true witness among those in the holy chain that stretched straight from Jerusalem to the Danish capital.

This little speech happened to wound a certain person in town, who felt as if he had been stabbed by a knife. This person felt outraged by what he viewed as a violation of eternal truth, and he was the same man whom the whole city had rejected and no longer took seriously. Now he wanted to know, if this really was the truth about the appeasing bishop, who then was the Eternal and incarnated One? And for that matter, what had his own lonely life been other than a futile fighting of windmills and ideals where the only truth and reality existed in his own bruised soul and offended thoughts? Were there more truths than the one single truth? If there were many truths, then he had no right from above to be a witness for Him who was absolute Truth.

And so it happened that the churchgoing part of town came face-to-face with the incredible, a catastrophe which would disturb the congregation's peace of soul and interrupt their daily routines for weeks. Whenever they opened their newspaper *Fædrelandet*, they were confronted with an article by *him*, the enigmatic and rejected one who walked through the streets looking like a vegetable. The articles read as if they were written in red blood, and every word was an offense which acted as a personal insult to the public spirit and the Church. Not a single high-ranking official could avoid feeling this blow to his innermost being. Pastors felt scandalized on behalf of their congregations, the new bishop was so offended, he withdrew into himself and became as silent as a wall. The whole town talked about nothing but the sacrilege being committed before their very eyes.

Even the public security within the Church was being threatened to its core. Every single line in these horribly injust articles acted as an insult to the public's sense of decency. Every single sentence was nothing short of an attack on decent people's harmless lives. Every single column was a malicious attempt to smash in church windows, as well as every plate of colored glass in every home, through all of which fate and God were being viewed. The broken pieces lay scattered everywhere. There was hope's green shards, optimism's red, and even friendship's purple. Catastrophe, catastrophe! What a catastrophe! This sacrilege seemed so great, it would be impossible to ever return to the old ways. For six months the people and the Church were like a besieged city.

Every person in town wanted the law to come down hard on this presumptuous man who had dared to alarm and attack a law-abiding community. Everyone wanted him deported to the island of Christiansø, and to stay there and suffer for the rest of his life. ∎

(Svend Leopold, *Søren Kierkegaard: Geniets tragedie*, Gyldendal, Copenhagen 1932)

Top: Our Lady's cathedral with the university in front. Bottom: The bishop's residence across the street, with the Reformation Monument in front.

A Philosophy Applied

Interview with Per Lønning

Per Lønning wrote his Ph.D. dissertation on "Contemporaneousness in Kierkegaard's Understanding of Christianity." He has twice been appointed bishop in the Lutheran Church of Norway. He has also been a member of the central committee of the World Council of Churches and a member of the Norwegian Parliament.

Kierkegaard talks about repetition. *This applies in a special way to you. Tell how.*
In my own life, and with great help from Kierkegaard, I have experienced what he calls *repetition*, a concept which has its classic expression in Kierkegaard's *Fear and Trembling*, where he discusses Abraham's sacrifice of Isaac. God had commanded Abraham to give back Isaac by sacrificing him, but at the crucial moment Isaac is given back to Abraham by means of the Absurd. I have similarly, received back my ministry as a bishop twelve years after I had had to resign.

Why wa this sacrifice necessary?
I felt I had to resign from the diocese because the state, with which the Church was then, even more than today, legally affiliated, legalized abortion without first being willing to discuss the questions concerning human rights which the Church had raised. I was criticized for my decision, but after much consideration I chose to resign because I felt this was God's way in my particular situation.

How did you answer your critics?
I said that my calling was to act the way I did in this specific situation; that the only testimony I could give of equal weight to the seriousness of the matter, was to resign. People asked me, "What will you do?" and I had to honestly say, "I don't know. I am available to God

> *My calling was to act the way I did in this specific situation; this was the only testimony I could give of equal weight to the seriousness of the matter.*

and my Church. I must wait and see where God takes me." Twelve years later, after a period when surprising and challenging calls led me to various services in domestic and international church life, I was called back by the Church to resume my work as bishop. At that point I realized it was God's calling that I continue this ministry.

You mentioned the Absurd. What was the Absurd in your case?
Abraham was seemingly utterly inconsistent when he received Isaac back. What Kierkegaard calls *repetition* is this inconsistency that we must resign ourselves to God's will and see where He takes us. In Kierkegaard's particular case, he hoped to gain Regine back. That's why he claimed that, had he had faith, he would have stayed with her. What he probably meant was that, had he overcome his own fear of acting inconsistently and thus exposing himself to human contempt, he would have observed divine signals that his trial had ended and that God was ready to turn his sacrifice into gain.

Are you saying that you had this faith and that Kierkegaard did not, since you, contrary to Kierkegaard, received back that which you had sacrificed?
Faith is not something you have; it is something you receive. But while struggling with my scruples, I have found Kierkegaard to be a tremendous help. He has helped me toward a clearer understanding because he made me realize that, in the midst of a situation where I had to sacrifice everything, God would open up a future where I, on new and different terms, would receive back that which I had had to sacrifice.

You have studied Kierkegaard since your youth?
Yes, but it was not until this became real in my personal life that the issue in *Fear and Trembling* became important to me. My dissertation in 1954 was on Kierkegaard's concept of contemporaneousness which he expounds in *Philosophical Fragments* and *Practice in Christianity*. For Kierkegaard it was crucial to live contemporaneously with Christ. In other words, it is not enough to relate to a piece of history from the past; one must relate to Him here and now in the same way his contemporaries must believe the paradox that He was the One He said He was, despite what they actually saw with their eyes. In a way, in *Philosophical Fragments* Kierkegaard constructs the Christian faith from "scratch," without even using Christian terms. Under his pseudonym, Johannes Climacus, Kierkegaard argues that man is in untruth and that God must become God in time, in order for salvation to become a real gift, with no

> *Kierkegaard argues that man is in untruth, and that God must become God in time, in order for salvation to become a real gift, with no strings attached.*

63

strings attached. Whether we lived in Jesus' time, or are alive today – the situation is the same: we can only believe Him by encountering Him as being present in the paradox. In *Concluding Unscientific Postscript* this argument logically leads to Kierkegaard's famous contradiction that "subjectivity is truth" and "subjectivity is untruth." Not only does Christianity expose the fact that we do not have the truth in ourselves but are dependent on God's grace, it also offers us this understanding, not as a dictate rammed down our throats, but as a form of liberation awakening the innermost part of each of us. The Truth becomes our truth.

The theme of *Fear and Trembling* – the dilemma of whether it is morally justifiable in certain situations to do something that is "unethical" like Abraham sacrificing Isaac – did not concern me until later, when I was facing the moral dilemma of whether I should resign or not, because this involved not only myself but also my family, my diocese and good friends, all of whom might suffer personally as a result of my decision.

By choosing to resign, did you automatically cut yourself off from exercising your authority as a bishop?
In some cases, especially cases of social and ethical concern, there may come a point when all arguments are exhausted and all conclusions drawn, and there is simply nothing more to add. In my particular situation this meant that I had to emphasize the seriousness of the matter by stepping outside the establishment of society. Sometimes God may give a person a special command, and since I was the Church's spokesperson concerning abortion, it was understandable that I was the one who had to leave, without any security net under me. This was the truest testimony I could give at the time, and a choice like this has its price.

During the recent, international Kierkegaard conference in Copenhagen you gave an address entitled, "Kierkegaard – a stumbling block to Kierkegaardians." Do you think that Kierkegaard has become an establishment within the establishment?
I think we must be careful not to proclaim our agreement with Kierkegaard too hastily, for he really withdraws himself from our strategies and manipulations. I must say that I am fickle about the place awarded to Kierkegaard research and the status it has lately gained all over the world. Kierkegaard is the only author who, especially in his own city of Copenhagen, has suffered the fate of becoming an establishment within the theological establishment. This seems inconsistent with

> "In some cases, especially cases of social and ethical concern, there may come a point when all arguments are exhausted and all conclusions drawn, and there is simply nothing more to add.

> *For Kierkegaard, a Christian is one who follows Christ to the limits, to the cross, one who consciously says no to being merely an admirer or spectator.*

Kierkegaard's critique of the Church. At a conference like this we must ask ourselves whether we are truly in accordance with his appeal, his message within the message.

Does Kierkegaard have something to say to evangelical Christians in the 1990's?
Very much, although they may not be able to benefit from all of his various writings. In his speeches and in *Works of Love* especially, there is much that speaks to an average, Christian conscience. I would also like to recommend *Practice in Christianity*, especially for mature Christians. Some of Kierkegaard's other works are too philosophically advanced for an ordinary audience. But in general I must say that Kierkegaard covers a wide field, while at the same time staying true to his Christ-centeredness. On one hand he is uncompromisingly focused and on the other hand, fully open to the world. This, I think, must be an example to follow for any Christian.

What is it in Kierkegaard's message that we need as Christians today?
At this time, when prosperity theology is advancing, much of what Kierkegaard has to say is becoming more relevant than ever before. Kierkegaard's theology is a theology of the cross: you must die to yourself before you can receive the glory of God's kingdom. There is not much room for this in our contemporary kind of success Christianity. For Kierkegaard, a Christian is one who follows Christ to the limits, to the cross, one who consciously says *no* to being merely an admirer or spectator. ■

The Inner Life

Kierkegaard's life was one long breath of prayer

"It was quite right once to sink into God and then remain there, but since man is a finite being, to pray means continual striving to achieve the true inwardness of prayer."
Journals 1845

"To pray is . . . to breathe, and possibility is for the self what oxygen is for breathing." The Sickness Unto Death

Kierkegaard is rarely quoted in sermons on prayer. Yet his life was more than anything a sermon with prayer as its prevalent theme. As much as philosophy is a way of learning to live, prayer is the way of learning to die. When Kierkegaard was on his deathbed, his lifelong friend Emil Boesen asked whether he could pray with peace in his heart. Kierkegaard answered, "Yes, that I can. First of all I pray that my sins may be forgiven me, that everything may be forgiven. Then I pray that I may be free from despair in death, and the words often occur to me where it is said that death should be pleasing to God. And so I pray for what I so much desire, which is that I may know a little beforehand when death is to come." *(Journals)* For Kierkegaard, prayer was the Christian's way of anticipating death and eternal life, the "greatest earthly happiness" a person could experience.

Although Kierkegaard was reluctant to talk about his personal devotional life ("It is too true for me to be able to talk about," he confided to his journal), he did write many prayers in his journals and edifying discourses, some of which are beautiful accounts of a pilgrim's persistent progress with God. In his book *The Prayers of Kierkegaard*, Perry LeFevre lists close to a hundred of these prayers. They are the deepest recorded testimony of Kierkegaard's struggle with depression and his prevailing with God over doubt and despair through increased faith and inwardness: "Teach me, O God, not to torture myself, not to make a martyr out of myself through stifling reflection, but rather teach me to breathe deeply in faith." *(Journals and Papers)* The title of one of his discourses, "The Righteous Man Strives in Prayer with God and Conquers in That God Conquers," could well serve as the headline for his life. It is interesting, as LeFevre observes, that in the months prior to the *Corsair* controversy, Kierkegaard was especially devoted to prayer.

The *Journals* bear witness to the fact that Kierkegaard prayed frequently for the people and needs around him. But more than anything, Kierkegaard considered prayer as a means of attaining purity of heart and inwardness with God. Prayer was his way to examine motives and surrender the soul to God in "tranquil abandonment." Whenever he approached God in this way, especially during crises in his life, he always came away with an enormous gratitude to God. "He lets me weep before Him in silent solitude," he wrote in the journal, "pour forth and again pour forth my pain, with the blessed consolation of knowing that He is concerned for me - and in the meanwhile He gives that life of pain a significance which almost overwhelms me." Prayer was the weapon that fought back melancholy and doubt and soothed his heart to rest in God.

Although prayer has its victorious moments of power and joy, according to Kierkegaard, these moments are only secondary rewards for those pursuing a life of prayer. During the course of his own life, Kierkegaard came to realize that the true purpose of prayer is not for a man to conquer the world, but for God to conquer a man's heart. Prayer is an altar in the world, a place where everyone may come day and

Two things in particular occupy me: 1) that whatever the cost I should remain intellectually true in the Greek sense to my life's idea; 2) that religiously it should be as ennobling as possible. For the second I pray to God. Journals

The best help in all action is to pray; this is true genius. Then one never goes wrong. Journals

Prayer. . . really is a silent surrendering of everything to God because it is not quite clear to me how I should pray. Journals

That you are able at every moment to close your door and speak to God without an intermediary, without having to pay a heavy charge to appear before a great one, is this not a happiness?
Journals and Papers

A surprising thing happened to him. The more earnest he became in prayer, the less he had to say, and in the end he became quite silent.
Christian Discourses

night to surrender his heart in the intimate language of prayer. Prayer is the only language in which man's true identity is revealed. The more time one spends in this kind of prayer, the more one is becoming an authentic person. And as the years go by, prayer becomes increasingly more difficult, for a person of prayer comes to the increasing realization that prayer is not so much a means of getting rid of anxiety and misfortune, as a way of accepting and suffering through these states. So it is that a person begins his prayer by speaking to God in order to be heard - and he ends in silence in order to hear God speak. "The immediate person," says Kierkegaard in the *Journals*, "thinks and imagines that when he prays, the important thing, the thing he must concentrate upon, is that *God should hear* what *he is praying for*. And yet in the true eternal sense it is just the reverse: the true relation in prayer is not when God hears what is prayed for, but when *the person praying* continues to pray until he is *the one who hears*, who hears what God wills. The immediate person, therefore, uses many words and in so doing, makes demands while praying; the true man of prayer only *attends*." (*Journals*)

In other words, prayer is about forgetting oneself in order to remember God. Prayer is about giving up the temptation to manipulate God. Prayer is about no longer trying to move God, so that He can move in us. That is why the secret of prayer is surrender. Only those who come to God in prayer in total obedience, without withholding any part of their lives and beings, are fit for Christian prayer, for only they are prepared to receive God's answer, no matter what it may be. Prayer is the true archimedean point outside the immanent world from where God can move freely. "God created out of nothing," says Kierkegaard, "so when God wants to use a man He reduces him to nothing."

This means, prayer is not about asking God to rid us from pain and suffering and make us happy. Prayer means bearing suffering with joy as a sign that we are in a true relationship with God. Prayer is to die to self and the world, for it is precisely in the act of dying that we shall live. "By prayer," says Kierkegaard, "[a man] digs down always more to the heart of suffering; the nearer he approaches God in intimacy, the more he anchors himself in suffering." Why? Because God is a God who suffers, and suffering is God's way of staying lovingly anonymous in a suffering world. "I know," says Kierkegaard, "that in Thy love Thou sufferest with me more than I, O Infinite Love." Prayer is grounded in inward suffering. And from this suffering a new self shall emerge — a self that together with purity of heart, wills only one thing: the kingdom of God and a new creation. ∎

"God in Heaven, let me really feel my nothingness, not in order to despair over it, but in order to feel the more powerfully the greatness of Thy goodness."

"Father in Heaven! When the thought of Thee wakes in our hearts let it not awaken like a frightened bird that flies about in dismay, but like a child waking from its sleep with a heavenly smile."

"Father in Heaven! Hold not our sins up against us but hold us up against our sins, so that the thought of Thee when it wakens in our soul, and each time it wakens, should not remind us of what we have committed but of what Thou didst forgive, not of how we went astray but of how Thou didst save us!"

"My Lord God, give me once more the courage to hope; merciful God, let me hope once again, fructify my barren and infertile mind."

"Father in Heaven! Let us consider that whatever happens to us, this comes from Thee, and that of whatever comes from Thee nothing is able to harm us; no, no, it can only be to our benefit."

69

> **M**y dear reader, read aloud, if possible! If you do so, allow me to thank you for it; if you not only do it yourself, if you also influence others to do it, allow me to thank each one of them, and you again and again! By reading aloud you will gain the strongest impression that you have only yourself to consider, not me, who, after all, am "without authority," nor others, which would be a distraction.

For Self-Examination 1851

Part II

A KIERKEGAARD READER
Samples from Kierkegaard's works

EITHER/OR [1843]

The Anguish of Genius

What is a poet? An unhappy person who conceals profound anguish in his heart but whose lips are so formed that as sighs and cries pass over them they sound like beautiful music. It is with him as with the poor wretches in Phalaris's bronze bull, who were slowly tortured over a slow fire; their screams could not reach the tyrant's ears to terrify him; to him they sounded like sweet music. And people crowd around the poet and say to him, "Sing again soon" — in other words, may new sufferings torture your soul, and may your lips continue to be formed as before, because your screams would only alarm us, but the music is charming. And the reviewers step up and say, "That is right; so it must be according to the rules of esthetics." Now of course a reviewer resembles a poet to a hair, except that he does not have the anguish in his heart, or the music on his lips. Therefore, I would rather be a swineherd out on Amager and be understood by swine than be a poet and be misunderstood by people.

A Time Without Passion

Let others complain that the times are evil. I complain that they are wretched, for they are without passion. People's thoughts are as thin and fragile as lace, and they themselves as pitiable as lace-making girls. The thoughts of their hearts are too wretched to be sinful. It is perhaps possible to regard it as sin for a worm to nourish such thoughts, but not for a human being, who is created in the image of God. Their desires are staid and dull, their passions drowsy. They perform their duties, these mercenary souls, but just like the Jews, they indulge in trimming the coins a little; they think that, even though our Lord keeps ever so orderly an account book, they can still manage to trick him a little. Fie on them! That is why my soul always turns back to the Old Testament and to Shakespeare. There one still feels that those who speak are human beings; there they hate, there they love, there they murder the enemy, curse his descendants through all generations — there they sin.

Ridiculous Things

Of all ridiculous things the most ridiculous seems to me, to be busy — to be a man who is brisk about his food and his work. Therefore, whenever I see a fly settling, in the decisive moment, on the nose of such a person of affairs; or if he is spattered with mud from a carriage which drives past him in still greater haste; or the drawbridge opens up before him; or a tile falls down and knocks him dead, then I laugh heartily. And who, indeed, could help laughing? What, I wonder, do these busy folks get done? Are they to be classed with the woman who in her confusion about the house being on fire carried out the fire-tongs? What things of greater account, do you suppose, will they rescue from life's great conflagration?

Judge William: Choosing the Ethical Life

What, then, is it that I separate in my Either/Or? Is it good and evil? No, I only want to bring you to the point where this choice truly has meaning for you. It is on this that everything turns. As soon as a person can be brought to stand at the crossroads in such a way that there is no way out for him except to choose, he will choose the right thing. Therefore, if it should so happen that before you finish reading this somewhat lengthy exploration, which again is being sent to you in the form of a letter, you feel that the moment of choice has arrived, then throw away the remainder — do not bother with it; you have lost nothing. But choose, and you will see the validity inherent in so doing; indeed, no young girl can be as happy with her heart's choice as a man who has known how to choose. Consequently, either a person has to live esthetically or he has to live ethically. Here, as stated, it is still not a matter of a choice in the stricter sense, for the person who lives esthetically does not choose, and the person who chooses the esthetic after the ethical has become manifest to him is not living esthetically, for he is sinning and is subject to ethical qualifications, even if his life must be termed unethical. You see, this is, so to speak, the character indelebilis of the ethical, that the ethical, although it modestly places itself on the same level as the esthetic, nevertheless is essentially that which makes the choice a choice.

And this is what is sad when one contemplates human life, that so many live out their lives in quiet lostness; they outlive themselves, not in the sense that life's content successively unfolds and is now possessed in this unfolding, but they live, as it were, away from themselves and vanish like shadows. Their immortal souls are blown away, and they are not disquieted by the question of its immortality, because they are already disintegrated before they die. They do not live esthetically, but neither has the ethical become manifest to them in its wholeness; nor have they actually rejected it, and therefore they are not sinning either, except insofar as it is a sin to be neither one thing nor the other. Nor do they doubt their immortality, for the person who deeply and fervently doubts it on his own behalf is sure to find what is right. I say "on his own behalf," and it certainly is high time that someone warns against the magnanimous, gallant objectivity with which many thinkers think on behalf of all others and not on their own. If anyone calls what I am claiming here self-love, then I shall answer: That comes from having no idea of what this "self" is and from the futility of a person's gaining the whole world but losing himself, and also it is bound to be a poor argument that does not first and foremost convince the person who presents it.

Rather than designating the choice between good and evil, my Either/Or designates the choice by which one chooses good and evil or rules them out. Here the question is under what qualifications one will view all existence and personally live. That the person who chooses good and evil chooses the good is indeed true, but only later does this become manifest, for the esthetic is not evil but the indifferent. And that is why I said that the ethical constitutes the choice. Therefore, it is not so much a matter of choosing between willing good or willing evil as of choosing to will, but that in turn posits good and evil. The person who chooses the ethical chooses the good, but here the good is

REPETITION [1843]

altogether abstract; its being is thereby merely posited, and this by no means precludes that the one choosing cannot in turn choose evil even though he chose the good. Here you see again how important it is that a choice is made and that it does not depend so much upon deliberation as on the baptism of the will, which assimilates this into the ethical. The more time that passes by, the more difficult it becomes to choose, for the soul is continually in one part of the dilemma, and hence it becomes more and more difficult to work itself free. And yet this is necessary if a choice is to be made, and consequently extremely important if a choice means anything, and that this is the case I shall point out later.

⁕

A Letter with a Lesson from Job

My Silent Confidant:

The storms have spent their fury — the thunderstorm is over — Job has been censured before the face of humankind — the Lord and Job have come to an understanding, they are reconciled, "the confidence of the Lord dwells again in the tents of Job as in former days" — men have come to understand Job. Now they come to him and eat bread with him and are sorry for him and console him; his brothers and sisters, each one of them, give him a farthing and a gold ring — Job is blessed and has received everything double. This is called a repetition.

How beneficent a thunderstorm is! How blessed it is to be rebuked by God! As a rule, a person very easily becomes defiant when censured; when God judges, then he subsides, and, surrounded by the love that wishes to educate him, he forgets the pain.

Who could have imagined this ending? Yet no other ending is thinkable, and not this one either. When everything has stalled, when thought is immobilized, when language is silent, when explanation returns home in despair - then there has to be a thunderstorm. Who can understand this? and yet who can conceive of anything else?

Was Job proved to be in the wrong? Yes, eternally, for there is no higher court than the one that judged him. Was Job proved to be in the right? Yes, eternally, by being proved to be in the wrong before God.

So there is a repetition, after all. When does it occur? Well, that is hard to say

FEAR AND TREMBLING [1843]

in any human language. When did it occur for Job? When every thinkable human certainty and probability were impossible. Bit by bit he loses everything, and hope thereby gradually vanishes, inasmuch as actuality, far from being placated, rather lodges stronger and stronger allegations against him. from the point of view of immediacy, everything is lost. His friends, especially Bildad, know but one way out, that by submitting to the punishment he may dare to hope for a repetition to the point of overflowing. Job will not have it. With that the knot and the entanglement are tightened and can be untied only by a thunderstorm.

For me this story is an ineffable comfort. Was it not fortunate that I did not go through with your ingenious, admirable plan. Humanly speaking, it may have been cowardliness on my part, but perhaps now Governance can all the more easily help me.

My only regret is that I did not ask the girl to give me my freedom. I am sure that she would have done it. Indeed, who can grasp the generosity of a girl? And yet I cannot really regret it, for I know that I did what I did because I was too proud on her behalf.

If I had not had Job! I say no more lest I burden you with my everlasting refrain.

Your devoted

✥

Abraham's Sacrifice

"And God tempted Abraham and said to him, Take Isaac, your only son, whom you love, and go to the land of Moriah and offer him there as a burnt offering on a mountain that I shall show you."

It was early in the morning when Abraham arose, had the asses saddled, and left his tent, taking Isaac with him, but Sarah watched them from the window as they went down the valley — until she could see them no longer. They rode in silence for three days. On the morning of the fourth day, Abraham said not a word but raised his eyes and saw Mount Moriah in the distance. He left the young servants behind and, taking Isaac's hand, went up the mountain alone. But Abraham said to himself, "I will not hide from Isaac where this walk is taking him." He stood still, he laid his hand on Isaac's head in blessing, and Isaac kneeled to receive it. And Abraham's face epitomized fatherliness; his gaze was gentle, his words admonishing. But Isaac could not understand him, his soul could not be uplifted; he clasped Abraham's knees, he pleaded at his feet, he begged for his young life, for his beautiful hopes; he called to mind the job in Abraham's house, he called to mind the sorrow and the solitude. Then Abraham lifted the boy up and walked on, holding his hand, and his words were full of comfort and admonition. But Isaac could not understand him. Abraham climbed Mount Moriah, but Isaac did not understand him. Then Abraham turned away from him for a moment, but when Isaac saw Abraham's face again, it had changed; his gaze was wild, his whole being was sheer terror. He seized Isaac by the chest, threw him to the ground, and said, "Stupid boy, do you think I am your father? I am an

75

idolater. Do you think it is God's command? No, it is my desire." Then Isaac trembled and cried out in his anguish: "God in heaven, have mercy on me, God of Abraham, have mercy on me; if I have no father on earth, then you be my father!" But Abraham said softly to himself, "Lord God in heaven, I thank you; it is better that he believes me a monster than that he should lose faith in you."

❖

A King in Love

Suppose . . . that there was a king who loved a maiden of lowly station in life. This king's heart was unstained by the wisdom (loudly enough proclaimed) unacquainted with the difficulties that the understanding uncovers in order to trap the heart and that give the poets enough to do and make their magic formulas necessary. His resolution was easy to carry out, for every politician feared his wrath and dared not even to hint at anything. Every foreign country trembled before his power and dared not to refrain from sending a congratulatory delegation to the wedding. And no cringing courtier, groveling before him, dared to hurt his feelings lest his own head be crushed. So let the harp be tuned; let the poets' songs begin; let all be festive while erotic love celebrates its triumph, for erotic love is jubilant when it unites equal and equal and is triumphant when it makes equal in erotic love that which was unequal.

Then a concern awakened in the king's soul. Who but a king who thinks royally would dream of such a thing! He did not speak to anyone about his concern, for if he had done so, any one of his courtiers would presumably have said, "Your Majesty, you are doing the girl a favor for which she can never in her lifetime thank you adequately." No doubt the courtier would arouse the king's wrath, so that the king would have him executed for high treason against his beloved, and thereby would cause the king another kind of sorrow. Alone he grappled with the sorrow in his heart: whether the girl would be made happy by this, whether she would acquire the bold confidence never to remember what the king only wished to forget — that he was the king and she had been a lowly maiden. For if this happened, if this recollection awakened and at times, like a favored rival, took her mind away from the king, lured it into the inclosing reserve of secret sorrow, or if at times it walked past her soul as death walks across the grave — what would be the gloriousness of erotic love then! Then she would indeed have been happier if she had remained in obscurity, loved by one in a position of equality, contented in the humble hut, but boldly confident in her love and cheerful early and late. What a rich overabundance of sorrow stands here as if ripe, almost bending under the weight of its fertility, only awaiting the time of harvest when the thought of the king will thresh all the seeds of concern out of it. For even if the girl were satisfied to become nothing, that could not satisfy the king, simply because he loved her and because it would be far harder for him to be her benefactor than to lose her.

THE CONCEPT OF ANXIETY [1844]

The Dizziness of Freedom

Anxiety may be compared with dizziness. He whose eye happens to look down into the yawning abyss becomes dizzy. But what is the reason for this? It is just as much in his own eye as in the abyss, for suppose he had not looked down. Hence anxiety is the dizziness of freedom, which emerges when the spirit wants to posit the synthesis and freedom looks down into its own possibility, laying hold of finiteness to support itself. Freedom succumbs in this dizziness. Further than this, psychology cannot and will not go. In that very moment everything is changed, and freedom, when it again rises, sees that it is guilty. Between these two moments lies the leap, which no science has explained and which no science can explain. He who becomes guilty in anxiety becomes as ambiguously guilty as it is possible to become. Anxiety is a feminine weakness in which freedom faints. Psychologically speaking, the fall into sin always takes place in weakness. But anxiety is of all things the most selfish, and no concrete expression of freedom is as selfish as the possibility of every concretion. This again is the overwhelming factor that determines the individual's ambiguous relation, sympathetic and antipathetic. In anxiety there is the selfish infinity of possibility, which does not tempt like a choice but ensnaringly disquiets with its sweet anxiousness.

Anxiety That Leads to Faith

In one of Grimm's fairy tales there is a story of a young man who goes in search of adventure in order to learn what it is to be in anxiety. We will let the adventurer pursue his journey without concerning ourselves about whether he encountered the terrible on his way. However, I will say that this is an adventure that every human being must go through — to learn to be anxious in order that he may not perish either by never having been in anxiety or by succumbing in anxiety. Whoever has learned to be anxious in the right way has learned the ultimate.

If a human being were a beast or an angel, he could not be in anxiety. Because he is a synthesis, he can be in anxiety; and the more profoundly he is in anxiety, the greater is the man — yet not in the sense usually understood, in which anxiety is about something external, about something outside a person, but in the sense that he himself produces the anxiety. Only in this sense can the words be understood when it is said of Christ that he was anxious unto death, as well as the words spoken by Christ to Judas: What you are going to do, do quickly. Not even the terrifying verse that made even Luther anxious when preaching on it — "My God, my God, why hast thou forsaken me" — not even these words express suffering so profoundly. For the latter signify a condition in which Christ finds himself. and the former signify the relation to a condition that is not.

Anxiety is freedom's possibility, and only such anxiety is through faith absolutely

77

educative, because it consumes all finite ends and discovers all their deceptiveness. And no Grand Inquisitor has such dreadful torments in readiness as anxiety has, and no secret agent knows as cunningly as anxiety how to attack his suspect in his weakest moment or to make alluring the trap in which he will be caught, and no discerning judge understands how to interrogate and examine the accused as does anxiety, which never lets the accused escape, neither through amusement, nor by noise, nor during work, neither by day nor by night.

Whoever is educated by anxiety is educated by possibility, and only he who is educated by possibility is educated according to his infinitude. Therefore possibility is the weightiest of all categories. It is true that we often hear the opposite stated, that possibility is so light, whereas actuality is so heavy. But from whom does one hear such words? From wretched men who never knew what possibility is, and who, when actuality had shown that they were not good for anything and never would be, mendaciously revived a possibility that was very beautiful and very enchanting, while the foundation of this possibility was at the most a little youthful giddiness, of which they ought rather to be ashamed. Therefore this possibility that is said to be so light is commonly regarded as the possibility of happiness, fortune, etc. But this is not possibility. It is rather a mendacious invention that human depravity has dressed up so as to have a reason for complaining of life and Governance and a pretext for becoming self-important. No, in possibility all things are equally possible, and whoever has truly been brought up by possibility has grasped the terrible as well as the joyful. So when such a person graduates from the school of possibility, and he knows better than a child knows his ABC's that he can demand absolutely nothing of life and that the terrible, perdition, and annihilation live next door to every man, and when he has thoroughly learned that every anxiety about which he was anxious came upon him in the next moment — he will give actuality another explanation, he will praise actuality, and even when it rests heavily upon him, he will remember that it nevertheless is far, far lighter than possibility was. Only in this way can possibility be educative, because finiteness and the finite relations in which every individual is assigned a place, whether they be small, or everyday, or world-historical, educate only finitely, and a person can always persuade them, coax something else out of them, always bargain, always escape from them tolerably well, always keep himself a little on the outside, always prevent himself from absolutely learning something from them; and if he does this, the individual must again have possibility in himself and himself develop that from which he is to learn, even though in the next moment that from which he is to learn does not at all acknowledge that it is formed by him but absolutely deprives him of the power.

However, in order that an individual may thus be educated absolutely and infinitely by the possibility, he must be honest toward possibility and have faith. By faith I understand here what Hegel somewhere in his way correctly calls the inner certainty that anticipates infinity. When the discoveries of possibility are honestly administered, possibility will discover all the finitudes, but it will idealize them in the form of infinity and in anxiety overwhelm the individual until he again overcomes them in the anticipation of faith.

What I am saying here probably strikes many as obscure and foolish talk, because they pride themselves on never having been in anxiety. To this I would replay that one certainly should not be in anxiety about men and about finitudes, but only he who passes through the anxiety of the possible is educated to have no anxiety, not because he can escape the terrible things of life but because these always become weak by comparison with those of possibility. If, on the other hand, the speaker maintains that the great thing about him is that he has never been in anxiety, I will gladly provide him with my explanation: that it is because he is very spiritless.

If an individual defrauds possibility, by which he is to be educated, he never arrives at faith; then his faith will be the sagicity of finitude, just as his school was that of finitude. But men defraud possibility in every way, because otherwise every man, if he had merely put his head out of the window, would have seen enough for possibility to use in beginning its exercises. There is an engraving by Chodowiecki that represents the surrender of Calais as viewed by four persons of different temperaments, and the task of the artist was to mirror the various impressions in the facial expressions of the four. The most commonplace life no doubt has experiences enough, but the question is that of the possibility in the individuality who is honest with himself. It is told of one Indian hermit who for two years lived on dew that he once came to the city, tasted wine, and became addicted to drink. this story, like similar stories, can be understood in different ways. It may be regarded as comic, it may be regarded as tragic. But the individuality who is educated by possibility needs but one such story. In that very moment, he is absolutely identified with the unfortunate man; he knows no finite evasion by which he may escape. Now the anxiety of possibility holds him as its prey until, saved, it must hand him over to faith. In no other place can he find rest, for every other place of rest is mere chatter, although in the eyes of men it is sagacity. Therefore possibility is absolutely educative. In actuality, no man ever became so unhappy that he did not retain a little remnant, and common sense says quite correctly that if one is cunning, one knows how to make the best of things. But whoever took possibility's course in misfortune lost all, all, as no one in actuality ever lost it. Now, if he did not defraud the possibility that wanted to teach him and did not wheedle the anxiety that wanted to save him, then he would also receive everything back, as no one in actuality ever did, even though he received all things tenfold, for the disciple of possibility received infinity, and the soul of the other expired in the finite. In actuality, no one ever sank so deep that he could not sink deeper, and there may be one or many who sank deeper. But he who sank in possibility - his eye became dizzy, his eye became confused, so he could not grasp the measuring stick that Tom, Dick, and Harry hold out as a saving straw to one sinking; his ear was closed so he could not hear what the market price of men was in his own day, did not hear that he was just as good as the majority. He sank absolutely, but then in turn he emerged from the depth of the abyss lighter than all the troublesome and terrible things in life. However, I will not deny that whoever is educated by possibility is exposed to danger, not that of getting into bad company and going astray in various ways as are those educated by the finite, but the danger of a fall, namely, suicide. If at the beginning of his education he misunderstands the anxiety, so that it does not lead him to faith but away from faith, then he is lost. On the other hand, whoever is educated [by possibility] remains with anxiety; he does not permit himself to be deceived by its countless falsifications and accurately remembers the past. Then the assaults of anxiety, even though they be terrifying, will not be such that he flees from them. For him, anxiety becomes a serving spirit that against its will leads him where he wishes to go. Then, when it announces itself, when it cunningly pretends to have invented a new instrument of torture, far more terrible than anything before, he does not shrink back, and still less does he attempt to hold it off with noise and confusion; but he bids it welcome, greets it festively, and like Socrates who raised the poisoned cup, he shuts himself up with it and says as a patient would say to the surgeon when the painful operation is about to begin: Now I am ready. Then anxiety enters into his soul and searches out everything and anxiously torments everything finite and petty out of him, and then it leads him where he wants to go.

Solomon's Dream

Solomon's judgment is well enough known, it availed to discriminate between truth and deceit and to make the judge famous as a wise prince. His dream is not so well known.

If there is any pang of sympathy, it is that of having to be ashamed of one's father, of him whom one loves above all and to whom one is most indebted, to have to approach him backwards, with averted face, in order not to behold his dishonor. But what greater bliss of sympathy can be imagined than to dare to love as the son's wish prompts, and in addition to dare to be proud of him because he is the only elect, the singularly distinguished man, a nation's strength, a country's pride, God's friend, a promise for the future, extolled in his lifetime, held by memory in the highest praise! Happy Solomon, this was your lot! Among the chosen people (how glorious even to belong to them!) he was the King's son (enviable lot!), son of that king who was the elect among kings!

Thus Solomon lived happily with the prophet Nathan. The father's strength and the father's achievement did not inspire him to deeds of valor, for in fact no occasion was left for that, but it inspired him to admiration, and admiration made him a poet. But if the poet was almost jealous of his hero, the son was blissful in his devotion to the father.

Then the son one day made a visit to his royal father. In the night he awoke at hearing movement where the father slept. Horror seizes him, he fears it is a villain who would murder David. He steals nearer — he beholds David with a crushed and contrite heart, he hears a cry of despair from the soul of the penitent.

Faint at the sight he returns to his couch, he falls asleep, but he does not rest, he dreams, he dreams that David is an ungodly man, rejected by God, that the royal majesty is the sign of God's wrath upon him, that he must wear the purple as a punishment, that he is condemned to rule, condemned to hear the people's benediction, whereas the Lord's righteousness secretly and hiddenly pronounces judgment upon the guilty one; and the dream suggests the surmise that God is not the God of the pious but of the ungodly, and that one must be an ungodly man to be God's elect — and the horror of the dream is this contradiction.

While David lay upon the ground with crushed and contrite heart, Solomon arose from his couch, but his understanding was crushed. Horror seized him when he thought of what it is to be God's elect. He surmised that holy intimacy with God, the sincerity of the pure man before the Lord, was not the explanation, but that a private guilt was the secret which explained everything.

And Solomon became wise, but he did not become a hero; and he became a thinker, but he did not become a man of prayer; and he became a preacher, but he did not become a believer; and he was able to help many, but he was not able to help himself; and he became sensual, but not repentant; and he became contrite and cast down, but not again erect, for the power of the will had been strained by that which surpassed the strength of the youth. And he tossed through life, tossed about by life — strong, supernaturally strong, that is, womanishly weak in the stirring infatuations and marvellous inventions of imagination, ingenious in expounding thoughts. But there was a rift in his nature, and Solomon was like the paralytic who is unable to support his own body. In his harem he sat like a disillusioned old man, until desire for pleasure awoke and he shouted, "Strike the timbrels, dance before me, ye women." But when the Queen of the South came to visit him, attracted by his wisdom, then was his soul rich, and the wise answer flowed from his lips like the precious myrrh which flows from the trees of Arabia.

The Moment of Passion

If an existing individual were really able to transcend himself, the truth would be for him something final and complete; but where is the point at which he is outside himself? The I-am-I is a mathematical point which does not exist, and in so far there is nothing to prevent everyone from occupying this standpoint; the one will not be in the way of the other. It is only momentarily that the particular individual is able to realize existentially a unity of the infinite and the finite which transcends existence. This unity is realized in the moment of passion. Modern philosophy has tried anything and everything in the effort to help the individual to transcend himself objectively, which is a wholly impossible feat; existence exercises its restraining influence, and if philosophers nowadays had not become mere scribblers in the service of a fantastic thinking and its preoccupation, they would long ago have perceived that suicide was the only tolerable practical interpretation of its striving. But the scribbling modern philosophy holds passion in contempt; and yet passion is the culmination of existence for an existing individual — and we are all of us existing individuals. In passion the existing subject is rendered infinite in the eternity of the imaginative representation, and yet he is at the same time most definitely himself. The fantastic I-am-I is not an identity of the infinite and the finite, since neither the one nor the other is real; it is a fantastic rendezvous in the clouds, an unfruitful embrace, and the relationship of the individual self to his mirage is never indicated.

Searching for God

The existing individual who chooses to pursue the objective way [of getting to know God] enters upon the entire approximation-process by which it is proposed to bring God to light objectively. But this is in all eternity impossible, because God is a subject, and therefore exists only for subjectivity in inwardness. The existing individual who chooses the subjective way apprehends instantly the entire dialectical difficulty involved in having to use some time, perhaps a long time, in finding God objectively; and he feels this dialectical difficulty in all its painfulness, because every moment is wasted in which he does not have God. That very instant he has God, not by virtue of any objective deliberation, but by virtue of the infinite passion of inwardness. The objective inquirer, on the other hand, is not embarrassed by such dialectical difficulties as are involved in devoting an entire period of investigation to finding God — since it is possible that the inquirer may die tomorrow; and if he lives he can scarcely regard God as something to be taken along if convenient, since God is precisely that which one takes *a tout prix*, which in the understanding of passion constitutes the true inward relationship to God. . . .

Now when the problem is to reckon up on which side there is most truth, whether on the side of one who seeks the true God objectively, and pursues the approximate truth of the God-idea; or on the side of one who, driven by the infinite passion of his need of God, feels an infinite concern for his own relationship to God in truth (and to be at one and the same time on both sides equally, is as we have noted not possible for an existing individual, but is merely the happy delusion of an imaginary I-am-I): the answer cannot be in doubt for anyone who has not been demoralized with the aid of science. If one who lives in the midst of Christendom goes up to the house of God, the house of the true God, with the true conception of God in his knowledge, and prays, but prays in a false spirit; and one who lives in an idolatrous community prays with the entire passion of the infinite, although his eyes rest upon the image of an idol: where is there most truth? The one prays in truth to God, though he worships an idol; the other prays falsely to the true God, and hence worships in fact an idol.

Seventy Thousand Fathoms of Water

When subjectivity is the truth, the conceptual determination of the truth must include an expression for the antithesis to objectivity, a memento of the fork in the road where the way swings off; this expression will at the same time serve as an indication of the tension of the subjective inwardness. Here is such a definition of truth: An objective uncertainty held fast in an appropriation-process of the most passionate inwardness is the truth, the highest truth attainable for an existing individual. At the point where the way swings off (and where this is cannot be specified objectively, since it is a matter of subjectivity), there objective knowledge is placed in abeyance. Thus the subject merely has, objectively, the uncertainty; but it is this which precisely increases the tension of that infinite passion which constitutes his inwardness. The truth is precisely the venture which chooses an objective uncertainty with the passion of the infinite. I contemplate the order of nature in the hope of finding God, and I see omnipotence and wisdom; but I also see much else that disturbs my mind and excites anxiety. The sum of all this is an objective uncertainty. But it is for this very reason that the inwardness becomes as intense as it is, for it embraces this objective uncertainty with the entire passion of the infinite. In the case of a mathematical proposition the objectivity is given, but for this reason the truth of such a proposition is also an indifferent truth.

But the above definition of truth is an equivalent expression for faith. Without risk there is no faith. Faith is precisely the contradiction between the infinite passion of the individual's inwardness and the objective uncertainty. If I am capable of grasping God objectively, I do not believe, but precisely because I cannot do this I must believe. If I wish to preserve myself in faith I must constantly be intent upon holding fast the objective uncertainty, so as to remain out upon the deep, over seventy thousand fathoms of water, still preserving my faith.

Risking the Paradox

When the eternal truth is related to an existing individual it becomes a paradox. The paradox repels in the inwardness of the existing individual, through the objective uncertainty and the corresponding Socratic ignorance. But since the paradox is not in the first instance itself paradoxical (but only in its relationship to the existing individual), it does not repel with a sufficient intensive inwardness. For without risk there is no faith, and the greater the risk the greater the faith; the more objective security the less inwardness (for inwardness is precisely subjectivity), and the less objective security the more profound the possible inwardness. When the paradox is paradoxical in itself, it repels the individual by virtue of its absurdity, and the corresponding passion of inwardness is faith. But subjectivity, inwardness, is the truth; for otherwise we have forgotten what the merit of the Socratic position is. But there can be no stronger expression for inwardness than when the retreat out of existence into the eternal by way of recollection is impossible; and when, with truth confronting the individual as a paradox, gripped in the anguish and pain of sin, facing the tremendous risk of the objective insecurity, the individual believes. But without risk no faith, not even the Socratic form of faith, much less the form of which we here speak.

What now is the absurd? The absurd is — that the eternal truth has come into being in time, that God has come into being, has been born, has grown up, and so forth, precisely like any other individual human being, quite indistinguishable from other individuals. . . .

Christianity has declared itself to be the eternal essential truth which has come into being in time. It has proclaimed itself as the Paradox, and it has required of the individual the inwardness of faith in relation to that which stamps itself as an offense to the Jews and a folly to the Greeks — and an absurdity to the understanding. It is impossible more strongly to express the fact that subjectivity is truth, and that the objectivity is repellent, repellent even by virtue of its absurdity. And indeed it would seem very strange that Christianity should have come into the world merely to receive an explanation; as if it had been somewhat bewildered about itself, and hence entered the world to consult that wise man, the speculative philosopher, who can come to its assistance by furnishing the explanation. It is impossible to express with more intensive inwardness the principle that subjectivity is truth, than when subjectivity is in the first instance untruth, and yet subjectivity is the truth.

The Absurdity of Christianity

Suppose Christianity never intended to be understood; suppose that, in order to express this, and to prevent anyone from misguidedly entering upon the objective way, it has declared itself to be the paradox. Suppose it wished to have significance only for existing individuals, and essentially for existing individuals in inwardness, in the inwardness of faith; which cannot be expressed more definitely than in the proposition that Christianity is the absurd, held fast in the passion of the infinite. Suppose it refuses to be understood, and that the maximum of understanding which could come in question is to understand that it cannot be understood. Suppose it therefore accentuates existence so decisively that the individual becomes a sinner, Christianity the paradox, existence the period of decision. Suppose that speculation were a temptation, the most dubious of all. Suppose that the speculative philosopher is, not indeed the prodigal son, for so the anxious divinity would characterize only the offended individual whom he nevertheless continues to love, but is the naughty child who refuses to remain where existing individuals belong, namely, in the existential training school where one becomes mature only through inwardness in existing, but instead demands a place in the divine council chamber, constantly shouting that viewed eternally, divinely, theocentrically, there is no paradox.

Pilate's Problem

But whoever is neither cold nor hot is nauseating; and just as the hunter is ill-served by a weapon that misses fire at the crucial moment, so God is ill-served by misfiring individuals. Had not Pilate asked objectively what truth is, he would never have condemned Christ to be crucified. Had he asked subjectively, the passion of his inwardness respecting what in the decision facing him he had in truth to do, would have prevented him from doing wrong. It would then not have been merely his wife who was made anxious by the dreadful dream, but Pilate himself would have become sleepless. But when a man has something so infinitely great before his eyes as the objective truth, he can afford to set at naught his little bit of subjectivity, and what he as subject has to do. And the approximation-process of the objective truth is figuratively expressed in washing the hands, for objectively there is no decision, and the subjective decision shows that one was in error nevertheless, through not understanding that the decision inheres precisely in subjectivity.

Suppose, on the other hand, that subjectivity is the truth, and that subjectivity is an existing subjectivity, then, if I may so express myself, Christianity fits perfectly into the picture. Subjectivity culminates in passion, Christianity is the paradox, paradox and passion are a mutual fit, and the paradox is altogether suited to one whose situation is, to be in the extremity of existence. Aye, never in all the world could there be found two lovers so wholly suited to one another as paradox and passion, and the strife between them is like the strife between lovers, when the dispute is about whether he first aroused her passion, or she his. And so it is here; the existing individual has by means of the paradox itself come to be placed in the extremity of existence. And what can be more splendid for lovers than that they are permitted a long time together without any alteration in the relationship between them, except that it becomes more intensive in inwardness? And this is indeed granted to the highly unspeculative understanding between passion and the paradox, since the whole of life in time is vouchsafed, and the change comes first in eternity. . . .

It is just possible that Christianity is the truth; it is possible that there will sometime come a judgment, where the separation will turn on the relationship of inwardness to Christianity. Suppose then there came a man who had to say: "I have not indeed believed, but so much have I honored Christianity that I have employed every hour of my life in pondering it." Or suppose there came one of whom the accuser had to say: "He has persecuted the Christians," and the accused replied: "Aye, I admit it; Christianity has set my soul aflame, and I have had no other ambition than to root it from the earth, precisely because I perceived its tremendous power." Or suppose there came another, of whom the accuser would have to say: "He has abjured Christianity," and the accused replied: "Aye, it is true; for I saw that Christianity was such a power that if I gave it a little finger it would take the whole man, and I felt that I could not belong to it wholly." But then suppose there finally came a dapper Privatdocent with light and nimble steps, who spoke as follows: "I am not like these three; I have not only believed, but I have even explained Christianity, and shown that as it was expounded by the Apostles and appropriated in the early centuries it was only to a certain degree true; but that now, through the interpretation of speculative philosophy it has become the true truth, whence I must ask for a suitable reward on account of my services to Christianity." Which of these four must be regarded as in the most terrible position? It is just possible that Christianity is the truth; suppose that now when its ungrateful children desire to have it declared incompetent, and placed under the guardianship of speculative philosophy, like the Greek poet whose children also demanded that the aged parent be placed under a guardian, but who astonished the judges and the people by writing one of his most beautiful tragedies as a sign that he was still in the full possession of his faculties - suppose that Christianity thus arose with renewed vigor: there would be no one else whose position would become as embarrassing as the position of the Privatdocents.

✣

Love Your Neighbor

When it is said, "You shall love your neighbor as yourself," this contains what is presupposed, that every person loves himself. Thus Christianity, which by no means begins, as do those high-flying thinkers, without presuppositions, nor with a flattering presupposition, presupposes this. Dare we then deny that it is as Christianity presupposes? But on the other hand, is it possible for anyone to misunderstand Christianity, as if it were its intention to teach what worldly sagacity unanimously — alas, and yet contentiously — teaches, "that everyone is closest [naermest] to himself." Is it possible for anyone to misunderstand this, as if it were Christianity's intention to proclaim self-love as a prescriptive right? Indeed, on the contrary, it is Christianity's intention to wrest self-love away from us human beings.

In other words, this is implied in loving oneself; but if one is to love the neighbor *as oneself*, then the commandment, as with a pick, wrenches open the lock of self-love and wrests it away from a person. If the commandment about loving the neighbor were expressed in any other way than with this little phrase, *as yourself*, which simultaneously is so easy to handle and yet has the elasticity of eternity, the commandment would leges in relation to him or is able to claim something from him. If someone with this view asks, "Who is my neighbor?" then that reply of Christ to the Pharisee will contain an answer only in a singular way, because in the answer the question is actually first turned around, whereby the meaning is: how is a person to ask the question. That is, after having told the parable of the merciful Samaritan, Christ says to the Pharisee (Luke 10:36), "Which of these three seems to you to have been the neighbor to the man who had fallen among robbers?" and the Pharisee answers correctly, "The one who showed mercy on him"— that is, by acknowledging your duty you easily discover who your neighbor is. The Pharisee's answer is contained in Christ's question, which by its form compelled the Pharisee to answer in that way. The one to whom I have a duty is my neighbor, and when I fulfill my duty I show that I am a neighbor. Christ does not speak about knowing the neighbor but about becoming a neighbor oneself, about showing oneself to be a neighbor just as the Samaritan showed it by his mercy. By this he did not show that the assaulted man was his neighbor but that he was a neighbor of the one assaulted. The Levite and the priest were in a stricter sense the victim's neighbor, but they wished to ignore it. The Samaritan, on the other hand, who because of prejudice was predisposed to misunderstanding, nevertheless correctly understood that he was a neighbor of the assaulted man. To choose a beloved, to find a friend, yes, this is a complicated business, but one's neighbor is easy to recognize, easy to find if only one will personally — acknowledge one's duty.

The commandment said, "You shall love your neighbor as yourself," but if the commandment is properly understood it also says the opposite: *You shall love yourself in the right way*. Therefore, if anyone is unwilling to learn from Christianity to love himself in the right way, he cannot love the neighbor either. He can perhaps hold together with another or a few other persons, "through thick and thin," as it is called, but this is by no means loving the neighbor. To love yourself in the right way and to love the neighbor correspond perfectly to one another; fundamentally they are one and the same thing. When the Law's *as yourself* has wrested from you the self-love that Christianity sadly enough must presuppose to be in every human being, then you have actually learned to love yourself. The Law is therefore: You shall love yourself in the same way as you love your neighbor when you love him as yourself. Whoever has any knowledge of people will certainly admit that just as he has often wished to be able to move them to relinquish self-love, he has also had to wish that it were possible to teach them to love themselves. When the bustler wastes his time and powers in the service of futile, inconsequential pursuits, is this not because he has not learned rightly to love himself? When the light-minded person throws himself almost like a nonentity into the folly of the moment and makes nothing of it, is this not because he does not know how to love himself rightly? When the depressed person desires to be rid of life, indeed, of himself, is this not because he is unwilling to learn earnestly and rigorously to love himself? When someone surrenders to despair because the world or another person has faithlessly left him betrayed, what then is his fault (his innocent suffering is not referred to here) except not loving himself in the right way? When someone self-tormentingly thinks to do God a service by torturing himself, what is his sin except not willing to love himself in the right way? And if, alas, a person presumptuously lays violent hands upon himself, is not his sin precisely this, that he does not rightly love himself in the sense in which a person ought to love himself?

Oh, there is a lot of talk in the world about treachery and faithlessness, and, God help us, it is unfortunately all too true, but still let us never because of this forget that the most dangerous traitor of all is the one every person has within himself. This treachery, whether it consists in selfishly loving oneself or consists in selfishly not willing to love oneself in the right way — this treachery is admittedly a secret. No cry is raised as it usually is in the case of treachery and faithlessness. But is it not therefore all the more important that Christianity's doctrine should be brought to mind again and again, that a person shall love his neighbor as himself, that is, as he ought to love himself?

The Two Artists

Suppose there were two artists, and the one said, "I have travelled much and seen much in the world, but I have sought in vain to find a man worth painting. I have found no face with such perfection of beauty that I could make up my mind to paint it. In every face I have seen one or another little fault. Therefore I seek in vain." Would this indicate that this artist was a great artist? On the other hand, the second one said, "Well, I do not pretend to be a real artist; neither have I travelled in foreign lands. But remaining in the little circle of men who are closest to me, I have not found a face so insignificant or so full of faults that I still could not discern in it a more beautiful side and discover something glorious. Therefore I am happy in the art I practice. It satisfies me without my making any claim to being an artist." Would this not indicate that precisely this one was the artist, one who by bringing a certain something with him found then and there what the much-travelled artist did not find anywhere in the world, perhaps because he did not bring a certain something with him! Consequently the second of the two was the artist. Would it not be sad, too, if what is intended to beautify life could only be a curse upon it, so that <u>art</u>, instead of making life beautiful for us, only fastidiously discovers that not one of us is beautiful. Would it not be sadder still, and still more confusing, if love also should

THE POINT OF VIEW [1848]

be only a curse because its demand could only make it evident that none of us is worth loving, instead of love's being recognized precisely by its loving enough to be able to find some lovableness in all of us, consequently loving enough to be able to love all of us.

✥

The Art of Christian Communication

An illusion can never be destroyed directly, and only by indirect means can it be radically removed. If it is an illusion that all are Christians — and if there is anything to be done about it, it must be done indirectly, not by one who vociferously proclaims himself an extraordinary Christian, but by one who, better instructed, is ready to declare that he is not a Christian at all. That is, one must approach from behind the person who is under an illusion. Instead of wishing to have the advantage of being oneself that rare thing, a Christian, one must let the prospective captive enjoy the advantage of being the Christian, and for one's own part have resignation enough to be the one who is far behind him — otherwise one will certainly not get the man out of his illusion, a thing which is difficult enough in any case. . . .

This is the secret of the art of helping others. Any one who has not mastered this is himself deluded when he proposes to help others. In order to help another effectively I must understand more than he — yet first of all surely I must understand what he understands. If I do not know that, my greater understanding will be of no help to him. If, however, I am disposed to plume myself on my greater understanding, it is because I am vain or proud, so that at bottom, instead of benefiting him, I want to be admired. But all true effort to help begins with self-humiliation: the helper must first humble himself under him he would help, and therewith must understand that to help does not mean to be a sovereign but to be a servant, that to help does not mean to be ambitious but to be patient, that to help means to endure for the time being the imputation that one is in the wrong and does not understand what the other understands. . . . And remember, serious and stern as you are, that if you cannot humble yourself, you are not genuinely serious. Be the amazed listener who sits and hears what the other finds the more delight in telling you because you listen with amazement. But above all do not forget one thing, the purpose you have in mind, the fact that it is the religious you must bring forward. . . .

If you can do that, if you can find exactly the place where the other is and begin there, you may perhaps have the luck to lead him to the place where you are.

For to be a teacher does not mean simply to affirm that such a thing is so, or to deliver a lecture, &c. No, to be a teacher in the right sense is to be a learner. Instruction begins when you, the teacher, put yourself in his place so that you may understand what he understands and in the way he understands it, in case you have not understood it before. Or if you have understood it before, you allow him to subject you to an examination so that he may be sure you know your part. This is the instruction. Then the beginning can be made in another sense.

To Witness for the Truth

The crowd is untruth. Therefore was Christ crucified, because, although He addressed Himself to all, He would have no dealings with the crowd, because He would not permit the crowd to aid Him in any way, because in this regard He repelled people absolutely, would not found a party, did not permit balloting, but would be what He is, the Truth, which relates itself to the individual. — And hence every one who truly would serve the truth is *eo ipso*, in one way or another, a martyr. If it were possible for a person in his mother's womb to make the decision to will to serve the truth truly, then, whatever his martyrdom turns out to be, he is *eo ipso* from his mother's womb a martyr. For it is not so great a trick to win the crowd. All that is needed is some talent, a certain dose of falsehood, and a little aquaintance with human passions. But no witness for the truth . . . dare become engaged with the crowd. The witness for the truth - who naturally has nothing to do with politics and must above everything else be most vigilantly on the watch not to be confounded with the politician - the God-fearing work of the witness to the truth is to engage himself if possible with all, but always individually, talking to every one severally on the streets and lanes . . . in order to disintegrate the crowd, or to talk even to the crowd, though not with the intent of forming a crowd, but rather with the hope that one or another individual might return from his assemblage and become a single individual.

Man is spirit

A human being is spirit. But what is spirit? Spirit is the self. But what is the self? The self is a relation that relates itself to itself or is the relation's relating itself to itself in the relation; the self is not the relation but is the relation's relating itself to itself. A human being is a synthesis of the infinite and the finite, of the temporal and the eternal, of freedom and necessity, in short, a synthesis. A synthesis is a relation between two. Considered in this way, a human being is still not a self.

In the relation between two, the relation is the third as a negative unity, and the two relate to the relation and in the relation to the relation; thus under the qualification of the psychical the relation between the psychical and the physical is a relation. If, however, the relation relates itself to itself, this relation is the positive third, and this is the self.

Such a relation that relates itself to itself, a self, must either have established itself or have been established by another.

If the relation that relates itself to itself has been established by another, then the relation is indeed the third, but this relation, the third, is yet again a relation and relates itself to that which established the entire relation.

The human self is such a derived,

established relation, a relation that relates itself to itself and in relating itself to itself relates itself to another. This is why there can be two forms of despair in the strict sense. If a human self had itself established itself, then there could be only one form: not to will to be oneself, to will to do away with oneself, but there could not be the form: in despair to will to be oneself. This second formulation is specifically the expression for the complete dependence of the relation (of the self), the expression for the inability to the self to arrive at or to be in equilibrium and rest by itself, but only, in relating itself to itself, by relating itself to that which has established the entire relation. Yes, this second form of despair (in despair to will to be oneself) is so far from designating merely a distinctive kind of despair that, on the contrary, all despair ultimately can be traced back to and be resolved in it. If the despairing person is aware of his despair, as he thinks he is, and does not speak meaninglessly of it as of something that is happening to him (somewhat as one suffering from dizziness speaks in nervous delusion of a weight on his head or of something that has fallen down on him, etc., a weight and a pressure that nevertheless are not something external but a reverse reflection of the internal) and now with all his power seeks to break the despair by himself and by himself alone — he is still in despair and with all his presumed effort only works himself all the deeper into deeper despair. The misrelation of despair is not a simple misrelation but a misrelation in a relation that relates itself to itself and has been established by another, so that the misrelation in that relation which is for itself also reflects itself infinitely in the relation to the power that established it.

The formula that describes the state of the self when despair is completely rooted out is this: in relating itself to itself and in willing to be itself, the self rests transparently in the power that established it.

Despair as Active Possibility

Is despair an excellence or a defect? Purely dialectically, it is both. If only the abstract idea of despair is considered, without any thought of someone in despair, it must be regarded as a surpassing excellence. The possibility of this sickness is man's superiority over the animal, and this superiority distinguishes him in quite another way than does his erect walk, for it indicates infinite erectness or sublimity, that he is spirit. The possibility of this sickness is man's superiority over the animal; to be aware of this sickness is the Christian's superiority over the natural man; to be cured of this sickness is the Christian's blessedness.

Consequently, to be able to despair is an infinite advantage, and yet to be in despair is not only the worst misfortune and misery — no, it is ruination. Generally this is not the case with the relation between possibility and actuality. If it is an excellence to be able to be this or that, then it is an even greater excellence to be that; in other words, to be is like an ascent when compared with being able to be. With respect to despair, however, to be is like a descent when compared with being able to be; the descent is as

THE SICKNESS UNTO DEATH [1849]

infinitely low as the excellence of possibility is high. Consequently, in relation to despair, not to be in despair is the ascending scale. but here again this category is ambiguous. Not to be in despair is not the same as not being lame, blind, etc. If not being in despair signifies neither more nor less than not being in despair, then it means precisely to be in despair. Not to be in despair must signify the destroyed possibility of being able to be in despair; if a person is truly not to be in despair, he must at every moment destroy the possibility. This is generally not the case in the relation between actuality and possibility. Admittedly, thinkers say that actuality is annihilated possibility, but that is not entirely true; it is the consummated, the active possibility. Here, on the contrary, the actuality (not to be in despair) is the impotent, destroyed possibility, which is why it is also a negation; although actuality in relation to possibility is usually a corroboration, here it is a denial.

The Root of Despair

An individual in despair despairs over something. So it seems for a moment, but only for a moment; in the same moment the true despair or despair in its true form shows itself. In despairing over something, he really despaired over himself, and now he wants to be rid of himself. For example, when the ambitious man whose slogan is "Either Caesar or nothing" does not get to be Caesar, he despairs over it. But this also means something else: precisely because he did not get to be Caesar, he now cannot bear to be himself. Consequently he does not despair because he did not get to be Caesar but despairs over himself because he did not get to be Caesar. This self, which, if it had become Caesar, would have been in seventh heaven (a state, incidentally, that in another sense is just as despairing), this self is now utterly intolerable to him. In a deeper sense, it is not his failure to become Caesar that is intolerable, but it is this self that did not become Caesar that is intolerable; or, to put it even more accurately, what is intolerable to him is that he cannot get rid of himself. If he had become Caesar, he would despairingly get rid of himself, but he did not become Caesar and cannot despairingly get rid of himself. Essentially, he is just as despairing, for he does not have his self, is not himself. He would not have become himself by become Caesar but would have been rid of himself, but he did not become Caesar and cannot despairingly get rid of himself. Essentially, he is just as despairing, for he does not have his self, is not himself. He would not have become himself by becoming Caesar but would have been rid of himself, and by not becoming Caesar he despairs over not being able to get rid of himself. Thus it is superficial for someone (who probably has never seen anyone in despair, not even himself) to say of a person in despair: He is consuming himself. But his is precisely what he in his despair [wants] and this is precisely what he to his torment cannot do, since the despair has inflamed something that cannot burn or be burned up in the self.

Consequently, to despair over something is still not despair proper. It is the beginning, or, as the physician says of an illness, it has not yet declared itself. The next is declared despair, to despair over oneself. A young girl despairs of love, that is, she despairs over the loss of her beloved, over his death or his unfaithfulness to her. This is not declared despair; no, she despairs over herself. This self of hers, which she would have been rid of or would have lost in the most blissful manner had it become "his" beloved, this self becomes a torment to her if it has to be a self without "him." This self, which would have become her treasure (although, in another sense, it would have been just as despairing), has now become to her an abominable void since "he" died, or it has become to her a nauseating reminder that she has been deceived. Just try it, say to such a girl, "You are consuming yourself," and you will hear her answer, "O, but the torment is simply that I cannot do that."

To despair over oneself, in despair to will to be rid of oneself — this is the formula for all despair. Therefore the other form of despair, in despair to will to be oneself, can be traced back to the first, in despair not to will to be oneself, just as we previously resolved the form, in despair not to will to be oneself, into the form, in despair to will to be oneself. A person in despair despairingly wills to be himself. But if he despairingly wills to be himself, he certainly does not want to be rid of himself. Well, so it seems, but upon closer examination it is clear that the contradiction is the same. The self that he despairingly wants to be is a self that he is not (for to will to be the self that he is in truth is the very opposite of despair), that is, he wants to tear his self away from the power that established it. In spite of all his despair, however, he cannot manage to do it; in spite of all his despairing efforts, that power is the stronger and forces him to be the self he does not want to be. But this is his way of willing to get rid of himself, to rid himself of the self that he is in order to be the self that he has dreamed up. He would be in seventh heaven to be the self he wants to be (although in another sense he would be just as despairing), but to be forced to be the self he does not want to be, that is his torment - that he cannot get rid of himself.

Socrates proved the immortality of the soul from the fact that sickness of the soul (sin) does not consume it as sickness of the body consumes the body. Similarly, the eternal in a person can be proved by the fact that despair cannot consume his self, that precisely this is the torment of contradiction in despair. If there were nothing eternal in a man, he could not despair at all; if despair could consume his self, then there would be no despair at all.

Such is the nature of despair, this sickness of the self, this sickness unto death. The despairing person is mortally ill. In a completely different sense than is the case with any illness, this sickness has attacked the most vital organs, and yet he cannot die. Death is not the end of the sickness, but death is incessantly the end. To be saved from this sickness by death is an impossibility, because the sickness and its torment — and the death — are precisely this inability to die.

This is the state in despair. No matter how much the despairing person avoids it,

This is the battle of faith, battling, madly, if you will, for possibility because possibility is the only salvation.

THE SICKNESS UNTO DEATH [1849]

no matter how successfully he has completely lost himself (especially the case in the form of despair that is ignorance of being in despair) and lost himself in such a manner that the loss is not at all detectable — eternity nevertheless will make it manifest that his condition was despair and will nail him to himself so that his torment will still be that he cannot rid himself of his self, and it will become obvious that he was just imagining that he had succeeded in doing so. Eternity is obliged to do this, because to have a self, to be a self, is the greatest concession, an infinite concession, given to man, but it is also eternity's claim upon him.

Not to Will to Be Oneself

This form of despair is: in despair not to will to be oneself. Or even lower: in despair not to will to be a self. Or lowest of all: in depair to will to be someone else, to wish for a new self. Immediacy actually has no self, it does not know itself; thus it cannot recognize itself and therefore generally ends in fantasy. When immediacy despairs, it does not even have enough self to wish or dream that it had become that which it has not become. The man of immediacy helps himself in another way: he wishes to be someone else. This is easily verified by observing immediate persons; when they are in despair, there is nothing they desire more than to have been someone else or to become someone else. . . . The man of immediacy does not know himself, he quite literally identifies himself with the clothes he wears, he identifies having a self by externalities. . . . So when the externals have completely changed for the person of immediacy and he has despaired, he goes one step further; he thinks something like this, it becomes his wish: What if I became someone else, got myself a new self. Well, what if he did become someone else? I wonder whether he would recognize himself. There is a story about a peasant who went barefooted to town with enough money to buy himself a pair of stockings and shoes and to get drunk, and in trying to find his way home in his drunken state, he fell asleep in the middle of the road. A carriage came along, and the driver shouted to him to move or he would drive over his legs. The drunken peasant woke up, looked at his legs and, not recognizing them because of the shoes and stockings, said: "Go ahead, they are not my legs."

The Battle of Faith

At this point, then, salvation is, humanly speaking, utterly impossible; but for God everything is possible! This is the battle of faith, battling, madly, if you will, for possibility, because possibility is the only salvation. When someone faints, we call for water, eau de Cologne, smelling salts; but when someone wants to despair, then the word is: Get possibility, get possibility, possibility is the only salvation. A possibility — then the person in despair breathes again, he revives again, for without possibility a person seems unable to breathe. At times the ingeniousness of the human imagination can extend to the point of creating possibility, but at last — that is, when it depends upon faith — then only this helps: that for God everything is possible.

Living in the Basement

However vain and conceited men may be, they usually have a very meager conception of themselves nevertheless, that is they have no conception of being spirit, the absolute that a human being can be; but vain and conceited they are — on the basis of comparison. Imagine a house with a basement, first floor, and second floor planned so that there is or is supposed to be a social distinction between the occupants according to floor. Now, if what it means to be a human being is compared with such a house, then all too regrettable the sad and ludicrous truth about the majority of people is that in their own house they prefer to live in the basement. Every human being is a psychical-physical synthesis intended to be spirit; this is the building, but he prefers to live in the basement, that is in sensate categories. Moreover, he not only prefers to live in the basement — no, he loves it so much that he is indignant if anyone suggests that he move to the superb upper floor that stands vacant and at his disposal, for he is, after all, living in his own house.

✣

Bringing Christianity Back into Christendom

This precisely is now the misfortune of Christendom, as for many, many years it has been, that Christ is neither the one thing nor the other, neither what He was when He lived on earth, nor what (as is believed) He shall be at His return, but one about whom in an illicit way, through history, people have learned to know something to the effect that He was somebody or another of considerable consequence. In an unpermissible and unlawful way people have become knowing about Christ, for the only permissible way is to be believing. People have mutually confirmed one another in the notion that by the aid of the upshot of Christ's life and the 1,800 years (the consequences) they have become acquainted with the answer to the problem. By degrees, as this came to be accounted wisdom, all pith and vigor was distilled out of Christianity; the tension of the paradox was relaxed, one became a Christian without noticing it, and without in the least noticing the possibility of offense. One took possession of Christ's doctrine, turned it about and pared it down, while He of course remained surety for its truth, He whose life had such stupendous results in history. All became as simple as thrusting a foot into the stocking. And quite naturally, because in that way Christianity became paganism. In Christianity there is perpetual Sunday twaddle about Christianity's glorious and priceless truths, its sweet consolation; but it is only too evident that Christ lived 1,800 years ago. The Sign of Offense and the Object of Faith has become the most romantic of all fabulous figures, a divine Uncle George. One does not know what it is to be offended, still less what it is to worship. What one especially praises in Christ is precisely what one would be most embittered by if one were contemporary with it, whereas now one is quite secure in reliance

preting and scholarly research and new scholarly research that is produced on the solemn and serious principle that it is in order to understand God's Word properly - look more closely and you will see that it is in order to defend oneself against God's Word. It is only all too easy to understand the requirement contained in God's Word ("Give all your goods to the poor." "If anyone strikes you on the right cheek, turn the left." "If anyone takes your coat, let him have your cloak also." "Rejoice always." "Count it sheer joy when you meet various temptations" etc.). It is all just as easy to understand as the remark "The weather is fine today," a remark that could become difficult to understand in only one way — if a literature came into existence in order to interpret it. The most limited poor creature cannot truthfully deny being able to understand the requirement — but it is tough for flesh and blood to will to understand it and to have to act accordingly. In my view, it is human for a person to shrink from letting the Word really gain power over him — if no one else will admit it, I admit that I do. It is human to pray to God to have patience if one cannot immediately do what one should but still promises to strive; it is human to pray to God to have mercy, that the requirement is too high for one — if no one else will admit it, I admit that I do. But nevertheless it is not human to give the matter a totally different turn: that I cunningly shove in, one layer after another, interpretation and scholarly research, and more scholarly research (much in the way a boy puts a napkin or more under his pants when he is going to get a licking), that I shove all this between the Word and myself and then give this interpreting and scholarliness the name of earnestness and zeal for the truth, and then allow this preoccupation to swell to such prolixity that I never come to receive the impression of God's Word, never come to look at myself in the mirror. It seems as if all this research and pondering and scrutinizing would draw God's Word very close to me; the truth is that this is the very way, this is the most cunning way, to remove God's Word as far as possible from me, infinitely further than it is from one who never saw God's Word, infinitely further than it is from one who became so anxious and afraid of God's Word that he cast it as far away as possible.

An even greater distance from what is required (to see oneself in the mirror), an even greater distance than never seeing the mirror, an even greater distance is this: to be able to sit entirely passive every single day, year in and year out — and observe the mirror.

✧

To Live as an Individual

The talk asks you, then, whether you live in such a way that you are conscious of being an "individual." The question is not of the inquisitive sort, as if one asked about that "individual" in some special sense, about the one whom admiration and envy unite in pointing out. No, it is the serious question, of what each man really is according to his eternal vocation, so that he himself shall be

Word or at least will confess to yourself that you, despite daily scholarly reading of it, are not reading God's Word, that you do not want anything to do with it at all. If you are not a scholar, there is less occasion to be mistaken; so straightway to the task, no delay in observing the mirror, but straightway to looking at yourself in the mirror.

But how is God's Word read in Christendom? If we were to be divided into two classes — since specific exceptions cannot be considered here — then one would have to say that the majority never read God's Word, a minority read it more or less learnedly, that is, nevertheless do not read God's Word but observe the mirror. To say it in other words, the majority regard God's Word as an obsolete ancient book one puts aside; a minority look upon God's Word as an extremely remarkable ancient book upon which one expends an amazing diligence, acumen, etc. — observing the mirror.

Imagine a country. A royal decree is issued to all public officials, subordinates — in short, to the whole population. What happens? A remarkable change takes place in everyone. Everybody turns into an interpreter, public officials become authors, and every blessed day an interpretation is published, one more learned, more penetrating, more elegant, more profound, more ingenious, more wonderful, more beautiful, more wonderfully beautiful than the other. Criticism, which is supposed to maintain an overview, can scarcely maintain an overview of this enormous literature; indeed, criticism itself becomes such a prolix literature that it is impossible to maintain an overview of the criticism: everything is interpretation — but on one read the decree in such a way that he complied with it. And not only this, that everything became interpretation — no, they also shifted the view of what earnestness is and made busyness with interpretations into real earnestness.

Suppose that this king is not a human king — because such a king would certainly understand that they were actually making a fool of him by twisting the matter in this way — but since a human king is dependent particularly on all his officials and subordinates, he would most likely be compelled to put the best face on it and pretend it was all right, so that the most elegant interpreter would be rewarded by being elevated to the nobility and the most profound would be honored with a medal etc.

Suppose that this king is omnipotent and consequently is not in an awkward position, even if all his officials and subordinates play him false. What do you suppose this omnipotent king will think of such a thing? I wonder if he would not say: That they do not obey the decree, I could forgive that. Furthermore, if they jointly presented to me a petition that I have patience with them or perhaps exempt them altogether from this decree that seems such a heavy burden to them — that I could forgive them. But this I cannot forgive — that they shift the view of what earnestness is.

And now God's Word! "My house is a house of prayer, but you have made it a robbers' den." And God's Word — what is it intended to be and into what have we changed it? All this interpreting and inter-

we are sober, and that it is precisely the unconditioned that would make us intoxicated. It is like that drunk man's saying "I am sober, but if I walked across that big square, the big square would make me drunk." "But, my good man, a big square is not something you drink; how can you get drunk from that? A sober person can walk across a big square very well without becoming drunk." In other words, the big square or walking across it makes manifest that the man is drunk, but the man says that it is the square that would do it, that he is sober. When one hugs the line of buildings, or at most walks down the middle of the way when it is through narrow alleys where the buildings really do hold on to one, then it is not perceived that one is drunk.

This is Christianity's view. It is not the unconditioned that makes one intoxicated, but it is the unconditioned that makes manifest that we are intoxicated — something we ourselves know well enough and therefore sagaciously stick to the finitudes, hug the line of buildings, stay in the alleys, and never venture out into the infinite. and it is Christianity's view that it is precisely the unconditioned that makes us sober after first making manifest that we are intoxicated. Ah, how sly we human beings are and how slyly we know how to use the language! We echo the truth as accurately as possible; fleetingly heard, it is as if we were saying the same thing. We leave out the little middle term "makes manifest," and then we say, "The unconditioned intoxicates" — this is thieves' jargon. Christianity says, "The unconditioned makes manifest that you are intoxicated, and there is only one thing that can make a person completely sober — the unconditioned."

When the apostles spoke on that first Pentecost Day, they were never more sober than on that very day. Their lives perfectly expressed the unconditioned; they had completely come to themselves as nothing in self-knowledge before God — that is, as mere instruments in his hand, lost to and liberated from every consideration, burned to spirit, completely sober — but mockery said, "They are full of sweet wine," and the sagacious, sensible, levelheaded, purely human point of view had to say: They are intoxicated.

⬥

God's Word as a Mirror

Alone with God's Word — this must one be, just as the lover wanted to be alone with the letter, for otherwise it would not be reading the letter from the beloved — and otherwise it is not reading God's Word or seeing oneself in the mirror. That is indeed what we should do and the first thing we should do if we are to look at ourselves with blessing in the mirror of the Word — we should not look at the mirror but see ourselves in the mirror. If you are a scholar, remember that if you do not read God's Word in another way, it will turn out that after a lifetime of reading God's Word many hours every day, you nevertheless have never read — God's Word. Then make the distinction (in addition to the scholarly reading), so that you will also really begin to read God's

JUDGE FOR YOURSELF [1851]

power whereas in the language of love it is Christ that holds him fast. So if anything further is required of him, God will surely let him understand; but this is required of everyone, that before God he shall candidly humble himself in view of the requirements of ideality. And therefore these should be heard again and again in their infinite significance. To be a Christian has become a thing of naught, mere tomfoolery, something which everyone is as a matter of course, something one slips into more easily than into the most insignificant trick of dexterity.

"But if the Christian life is something so terrible and frightful, how in the world can a person get the idea of accepting it?" Quite simply, and, if you want that too, quite in a Lutheran way: only the consciousness of sin can force one into this dreadful situation — the power on the other side being grace. And in that very instant the Christian life transforms itself and is sheer gentleness, grace, loving-kindness, and compassion. Looked at from any other point of view Christianity is and must be a sort of madness or the greatest horror. Only through the consciousness of sin is there entrance to it, and the wish to enter in by any other way is the crime of *lèse-majesté* against Christianity.

⁕

Intoxicated by Christendom

The truth of the matter is this. All of us human beings are more or less intoxicated. But we are like a drunk man who is not completely drunk so that he has lost his consciousness — no, he is definitely conscious that he is a little drunk and for that very reason is careful to conceal it from others, if possible from himself. What does he do then? He looks for something to sustain himself; he walks close to the buildings and walks erect without becoming dizzy — a sober man. But he would not dare to cross a large square, because then what he himself knows full well would become obvious — that he is intoxicated. This is how it is, spiritually understood, with us human beings. We have a suspicion about ourselves; we gradually become conscious that we are not really sober. But then sagacity and sensibleness and levelheadedness come to our aid and with their help we obtain something to sustain us — the finite. And then we walk, erect and confident, without staggering — we are completely sober. But if the unconditioned unconditionally were to catch sight of us — yet we avoid this glance, and that is why we conceal ourselves in finitude and among the finitudes in the same way as Adam hid among the trees. Or if we were to fix our eyes unconditionally upon the infinite — yet we keep ourselves away from this, and that is why we busily give our eyes errands in the service of finitude — if the unconditioned were to catch sight of us or we of the unconditioned, it would then become manifest that we are intoxicated.

This is the truth of the matter. But in our thieves' jargon we human beings express it differently; we maintain that we are sagacious, sensible, levelheaded people, that

99

And hence it is true, so true . . . when the wise and prudent man in the situation of contemporaneousness condemns Christ by saying, "He is literally nothing" — most certainly true, for He is the absolute. Christianity came into the world as the absolute — not for consolation, humanly understood; on the contrary, it speaks again and again of the sufferings which a Christian must endure, or which a man must endure to become and to be a Christian, sufferings he can well avoid merely by refraining from becoming a Christian.

There is an endless yawning difference between God and man, and hence, in the situation of contemporaneousness, to become a Christian (to be transformed into likeness with God) proved to be an even greater torment and misery and pain than the greatest human torment, and hence also a crime in the eyes of one's neighbors. And so it will always prove when becoming a Christian in truth comes to mean to become contemporary with Christ. And if becoming a Christian does not come to mean this, then all the talk about becoming a Christian is nonsense and self-deception and conceit, in part even blasphemy and sin against the Second Commandment of the Law and sin against the Holy Ghost.

For in relation to the absolute there is only one tense: the present. For him who is not contemporary with the absolute — for him it has no existence. And as Christ is the absolute, it is easy to see that with respect to Him there is only one situation: that of contemporaneousness. The five, the seven, the fifteen, the eighteen hundred years are neither here nor there; they do not change Him, neither do they in any wise reveal who He was, for who He is is revealed only to faith. . . .

The Christian Life

And what does all this mean? It means that everyone for himself, in quiet inwardness before God; shall humble himself before what it means in the strictest sense to be a Christian, admit candidly before God how it stands with him, so that he might yet accept the grace which is offered to everyone who is imperfect, that is, to everyone. And then no further; then for the rest let him attend to his work, be glad in it, love his wife, be glad in her, bring up his children with joyfulness, love his fellow men, rejoice in life. If anything further is required of him, God will surely let him understand, and in such case will also help him further; for the terrible language of the Law is so terrifying because it seems as if it were left to man to hold fast to Christ by his own

upon the upshot; and in reliance upon this proof from history, that He quite certainly was the great one, one draws the conclusion; ergo that was the right thing. This is to say, That is the right, the noble, the sublime, the true thing, if it was He that did it; this is the same as to say that one does not trouble oneself to learn to know in a deeper sense what it was He did, still less to try, according to one's slender ability, by God's help to imitate Him in doing the thing that is right and noble and sublime and true. For what that is one does not apprehend and may therefore in the situation of today form a judgment diametrically opposite to the truth. One is content to admire and praise, and may be (as was said of a scrupulous translator who rendered an author word for word and therefore made no meaning) "too conscientious," perhaps also too cowardly and too feeble of heart really to wish to understand.

Christendom has done away with Christianity, without being quite aware of it. The consequence is that, if anything is to be done, one must try again to introduce Christianity into Christendom.

How to Become a Christian

With this invitation to all them "that labor and are heavy laden" Christianity did not come into the world (as the parsons snivelingly and falsely introduce it) as an admirable example of the gentle art of consolation — but as the absolute. It is out of love God wills it so, but also it is God who wills it, and He wills what He will. He will not suffer Himself to be transformed by men and be a nice . . . human God: He will transform men, and that He wills out of love. He will have nothing to do with man's pert inquiry about why and why did Christianity come into the world: it is and shall be the absolute. Therefore everything men have hit upon relatively to explain the why and the wherefore is falsehood. Perhaps they have hit upon an explanation out of a human compassion of a sort, which thinks that one might chaffer about the price — for God presumably does not understand men, His requirements are exorbitant, and so the parsons must be on hand to chaffer. Perhaps they hit upon an explanation in order to stand well with men and get some advantage out of preaching Christianity; for when it is toned down to the merely human, to what has "entered into the heart of man," then naturally people will think well of it, and quite naturally also of the amiable orator who can make Christianity so gentle a thing — if the Apostles had been able to do that, people would also have thought well of the Apostles. But all this is falsehood, it is misrepresentation of Christianity, which is the absolute. But what, then, is the use of Christianity? It is, then, merely a plague to us! Ah, yes, that too can be said: relatively understood, the absolute is the greatest plague. In all moments of laxness, sluggishness, dullness, when the sensuous nature of man predominates, Christianity seems madness, since it is incommensurable with any finite wherefore. What is the use of it, then? The answer is: Hold thy peace! It is the absolute! And so it must be represented, viz. in such a way as to make it appear madness in the eyes of the sensuous man.

This consciousness is the fundamental condition for truthfully willing only one thing. For he who is not himself a unity is never really anything wholly and decisively; he only exists in an external sense — as long as he lives as a numeral within the crowd, a fraction within the earthly conglomeration.

conscious that he is following it; and what is even more serious, to ask it as if he were considering his life before God. This consciousness is the fundamental condition for truthfully willing only one thing. For he who is not himself a unity is never really anything wholly and decisively; he only exists in an external sense — as long as he lives as a numeral within the crowd, a fraction within the earthly conglomeration. Alas, how indeed should such a one decide to busy himself with the thought: truthfully to will only one thing!

Indeed it is precisely this consciousness that must be asked for. Just as if the talk could not ask in generalities, but rather asks you as an individual. Or, better still, my listener, if you would ask yourself, whether you have this consciousness, whether you are actively contemplating the occasion of this talk. For in the outside world, the crowd is busy making a noise. The one makes a noise because he heads the crowd, the many because they are members of the crowd. But the all-knowing One, who in spite of anyone is able to observe it all, does not desire the crowd. He desires the individual; He will deal only with the individual, quite unconcerned as to whether the individual be of high or low station, whether he be distinguished or wretched.

Each man himself, as an individual, should render his account to God. No third person dares venture to intrude upon this accounting between God and the individual. Yet the talk, by putting its question, dares and ought to dare, to remind man, in a way never to be forgotten, that the most ruinous evasion of all is to be hidden in the crowd in an attempt to escape God's supervision of him as an individual, in an attempt to get away from hearing God's voice as an individual. Long ago, Adam attempted this same thing when his evil conscience led him to imagine that he could hide himself among the trees. It may even be easier and more convenient, and more cowardly to hide oneself among the crowd in the hope that God should not be able to recognize one from the other. But in eternity each shall render account as an individual. That is, eternity will demand of him that he shall have lived as an individual. Eternity will draw out before his consciousness, all that he has done as an individual, he who had forgotten himself in noisy self-conceit. In eternity, he shall be brought to account strictly as an individual, he who intended to be in the crowd where there should be no such strict reckoning. Each one shall render account to God as an individual. The king shall render account as an individual; and the most wretched beggar, as an individual. No one may pride himself at being more than an individual, and no one despondently think that he is not an individual, perhaps because here in earth's busyness he had not as much as a name, but was named after a number.

For, after all, what is eternity's accounting other than that the voice of conscience is forever installed with its eternal right to be the exclusive voice? What is it other than that throughout eternity an infinite stillness reigns wherein the conscience may talk with the individual about what he, as an individual, of what he has done of good or of evil, and about the fact that during his life he did not wish to be an individual? What is it other than that within eternity there is infinite space so that each person, as an individual, is apart with his conscience? For in eternity there is no mob pressure, no crowd, no hiding place in the crowd, as little as there are riots or street fights! Here in the temporal order conscience is prepared to make each person into an individual. But here in the temporal order, in the unrest, in the noise, in the pressure of the mob, in the crowd, in the primeval forest of evasions, alas, it is true, the calamity still happens, that someone completely stifles the voice of his conscience — his conscience, for he can never rid himself of it. It continues to belong to him, or more accurately, he continues to belong to it. Yet we are not now talking about this calamity, for even among the better persons, it happens all too readily that the voice of conscience becomes merely one voice among many. Then it follows so easily that the isolated voice of conscience (as generally happens to a solitary one) becomes overruled — by the majority. But in eternity, conscience is the only voice that is heard. It must be heard by the individual, for the individual has become the eternal echo of this voice. It must be heard. There is no place to flee from it. For in the infinite there is no place, the individual is himself the place. It must be heard. In vain the individual looks about for the crowd. Alas, it is as if there were a world between him and the nearest individual, whose conscience is also speaking to him about what he as an individual has spoken, and done, and thought of good and of evil.

Do you now live so that you are conscious of yourself as an individual; that in each of your relations in which you come into touch with the outside world, you are conscious of yourself, and that at the same time you are related to yourself as an individual? Even in these relations which we may so beautifully style the most intimate of all, do you remember that you have a still more intimate relation, namely, that in which you as an individual are related to yourself before God?

Jesus, Our High Priest

"For we have not a high priest who is unable to feel compassion with our infirmities, but one who in all points was tried in like manner, yet without sin." (Hebrews 4:15)

Of this consolation speaks the sacred text which has been read. We have one who is able to feel compassion with our infirmities; and further, 'we have one who in all points was tried in like manner.' This actually is the condition for being able to have true compassion — for the compassion of the inexperienced and the untried is misunderstanding, most commonly it is for the sufferer a more or less grievous and painful misunderstanding — this is the condition; to be tried in like manner. When such is the case, one can entirely put oneself in the sufferer's place; and when in all points one is tried in like manner, one can put oneself entirely in the place of every sufferer. Such a High Priest we have, who can be compassionate; and that He must be compassionate you can perceive in fact that it was out of compassion He was in all points tried in like manner — it was indeed this which determined Him to come to the world, and again it was compassion, it was in order that He might truly be compassionate, that by His own free resolution He was in all points tried in like manner, He who entirely can put Himself, and can put Himself entirely, in your place, in mine, in yours.

About this we would speak in the brief moment prescribed.

Christ put Himself entirely in your place. He was God and became man — thus it was He put Himself in your place. This indeed is what true compassion is so fain to do, it so fain would put itself in the sufferer's place, in order to be able to give effectual consolation. But this at the same time is what human compassion is unable to do; only divine compassion is able — and God became man. He became man; and He became the man who of all men, absolutely all, suffered the most; never was there born, never shall there or can there be born a man who shall suffer as He did. Oh, what security for His compassion! Oh, what compassion to give such security! Compassion impels Him to throw open His arms for all sufferers. 'Come unto me', says He, 'all you that suffer and are heavy laden'; 'Come unto me,' says He; and He vouches for what He says, for (and this is the second call of the invitation) He was absolutely the greatest sufferer. Already it is something great if human compassion ventures to suffer almost as much as the sufferer — but out of compassion, for the sake of making the comfort sure, to suffer infinitely more than the sufferer . . . how great is that compassion! Human compassion, however, shrinks back with a shudder, it would rather remain sympathetically upon the secure seashore; or, if it ventures out, it is not willing to go by any means so far out as where the sufferer is — but what compassion, to go still farther out! You sufferer, what is it you do require? You require that the compassionate man shall put himself in your place — and He, Compassion itself, not only put Himself entirely in your place, but He had to suffer infinitely more than you! Ah, sometimes it seems perhaps to the sufferer in his despondency as if compassion were almost treacherously holding back a little — but here is compassion gone beyond thee in the suffering which is infinitely great!

The Publican's Confession

"And the publican stood afar off and would not even lift up his eyes unto heaven, but smote upon his breast, saying, God be merciful to me a sinner." (Luke 18:13)

Christianity came into the world and taught humility, but not all learned humility from Christianity, hypocrisy learned to change its mask and remained the same, or rather became even worse. Christianity came into the world and taught that you shall not in pride and vainglory seek out the highest seats at table, but sit in the lowest — and soon pride and vainglory were sitting vainly in the lowest seats at table, the same pride and vainglory . . . oh, no, not the same but still worse. So one might perhaps think it necessary to invert this passage and nearly all the Gospel passages, in consideration of the fact that hypocrisy and pride and vainglory and the worldly mind may want to invert the situation. But how would that be of any avail? It surely can only be the notion of morbid acumen and vain shrewdness to want to be so shrewd that by shrewdness misuse can be prevented. No, there is only one thing which overcomes, which more than overcomes, from the very beginning has endlessly overcome, all cunning, and that is the simplicity of the Gospel, which in its simplicity lets itself be deceived as it were, and yet in simplicity continues to be the simple. And this too is the edifying feature of the Gospel's simplicity, that the Evil could not prevail over it to the point of making it wish to be shrewd. Verily the Evil has won a victory, and a very serious victory, when it has prompted simplicity to wish to be shrewd . . . for the sake of making itself secure. For simplicity is made secure, eternally secure, only by letting itself in its simplicity be deceived, however clearly it sees through the deceit. . . .

The publican stood afar off. What does this mean? It means to stand by himself, alone with himself and God — thus you are far off, far from men, and far from God, with whom nevertheless you are alone; for in relation to a man it is true that when you are alone with him you are closest to him, when there are others present you are farther away; but in relation to God it is true that when there are several persons present it seems to you as though you were closer, and only when you are literally alone with Him you discover how far off you are. . . .

But the Pharisee who, in fact, according to the saying of the Scripture, 'stood by himself,' was he not standing afar off? Yes, if in truth he had stood by himself. The Gospel says that he stood by himself and thanked God 'that he was not like other men'. And where one has the other men with one, one does not stand by oneself. The Pharisee's pride consisted just in this, that he proudly used the other men to measure his distance from them, that before God he would not let go the thought of the other men, but would hold this thought fast, in order thus to stand proudly by himself . . . in contrast with other men; but this indeed is not to stand by oneself, least of all to stand by oneself before God.

The publican stood afar off. Being conscious of his guilt and crime, it was perhaps easier for him not to be tempted by the thought of the other men, who, as he must in fact admit, were better than he. About this, however, we will not presume to decide; but it is certain that he had forgotten all the others. He was alone, alone with the consciousness of his guilt and crime, he had entirely forgotten that there were in fact many other publicans beside him, it was as if he were the only one. He was not alone with his guilt in the face of a righteous man, he was alone before God — ah, that is to be afar off. For what is farther from guilt and sin that God's holiness? — and so, for one who is himself a sinner to be alone with this, is it not to be endlessly far off? . . .

The Gospel of Suffering

To follow then signifies going the same way as did the one whom one is following; consequently it signifies that he no longer visibly goes before. And in the same way it was necessary that Christ should go away, should die, before it could appear whether the disciple would follow him. It is many, many centuries since that happened, and yet it still happens almost constantly. For there is a time when Christ almost visibly walks by the side of the child, goes before it; but there also comes a time when He is taken away from the eye of the sensual imagination, so that it may appear in the earnestness of the decision, whether the adult will follow Him. . . .

To follow signifies, then, going entirely alone on the way the teacher went: to have no visible person with whom one can take counsel; to have to choose for one's self; to scream in vain, as the child screams in vain, for the mother dares not give it visible help; to despair in vain, for no human being can help, and heaven does not render visible assistance. But the fact of invisible assistance is precisely identical with learning to go alone, for it means learning to transform the mind into a likeness with that of the teacher, who nevertheless is not visibly present. To go alone! Moreover there is no one, no human being, who can choose for you, or in a final and decisive sense counsel you concerning the only important thing, counsel you decisively in the matter of your own eternal happiness; and however many might be willing to do this, it would only work to your injury. Alone! For after you have chosen, you will indeed find fellow pilgrims, but in the moment of decision, and every time there is peril of life, then you find yourself alone. No one, no one hears your ingratiating prayers or listens to your violent complaint — and yet there is abundant help and willingness in heaven; but it is invisible, so that precisely through it one may be helped to learn to go alone. This help does not come from outside and clasp your hand; it does not assist you as a kind-hearted man assists the sick; it does not lead you back by force when you have gone astray. No, only when you completely submit, completely give up all your own will and yield yourself from the depths of your heart and soul, does help come invisibly; but then you have precisely gone alone. . . .

So the one who chooses to follow Christ goes forth on the way. And then when he must also learn to know the world and what is of the world, its strength and his own weakness; when the strife with flesh and blood becomes frightening, the way hard, the enemies many, the friends none: then the pain wrings from him this sigh: "I am all alone!" My hearer: If a child who was learning to walk came crying to its mother and said: "I am walking alone" — then would not the mother say: "That is very wonderful, my child!" And so also with the one who follows Christ. Not only on this way is it true, as is usually said, that when the need is greatest the help is nearest at hand; no, here on this way, the greatest suffering is nearest to perfection. Do you know any other way where this is true? On every other way the converse is true: if sufferings come, then the heaviness predominates, moreover, in such a way that it may indicate that one had chosen the wrong way. On the way however, on which a man is following Christ, the highest suffering is the most glorious; when the pilgrim groans, he fundamentally esteems himself happy. Behold, if a man enters on some other, then he must in advance make himself familiar with the hazards of the way; perhaps things may go well and without accident, but perhaps so many obstructions may turn up that he can make no progress. On the way of self-denial, of following Christ, on the contrary, there is everlasting security on the way; on this way the "signs" of suffering are the joyful sign that one is advancing on the right way. But what joy is, however, greater than having dared to choose the best way, the way to the highest; and again, without this, what joy is equally as great as this: that the way is certain for all eternity. . . .

Only suffering trains for eternity; for eternity rests in faith, but faith is in obedience, and obedience is learned from suffering. There is no obedience without suffering, no faith without obedience, no eternity without faith. In suffering obedience is obedience, in obedience faith is faith, in faith eternity is eternity.

Affliction is the Way

Consider the joy in the thought: That it is not the way which is narrow, but the narrowness which is the way.

Consequently, the way of perfection leads through tribulations; and the subject of this discourse is, the joy for a sufferer in this thought. Hence the discourse is not this time the admonishing one of how one must walk on the way of affliction, but the joyful one for the sufferer, that the affliction is the how which indicates the way of perfection. In the spiritual sense the way is: how it is traveled. Which is then the way of perfection, that is, how does one walk on the way of perfection? One walks in afflictions. This is the first how; the second is, how one is to walk on the way of affliction. That this second must never be forgotten, either first or last, is certain enough, but neither must it be forgotten, on the contrary it must be remembered, moreover, the sufferer will be exactly strengthened for that purpose, when he has really found for himself the joy in the thought that the way of perfection is through afflictions — he who through being a sufferer is exactly in affliction.

When affliction is the way, then is this the joy: that it is hence immediately clear to the sufferer, and that he immediately knows definitely what the task is, so he does not need to use any time, or waste his strength, in reflecting whether the task should not be different. . . .

In the spiritual sense the way is this:

how it is traveled. Lo, when a poor wayfarer, whose feet are possibly sore, wincing at every step, almost drags himself forward on the way: then there is, even if it is never right for him to be envious, nevertheless, much good sense in the thought of envying the rich who ride by him in comfortable carriages. For the highway is completely indifferent to the distinction of how one travels it, and too it is undeniably pleasanter to drive in a comfortable carriage than to walk so oppressed. But in the spiritual sense the way is: how it is traveled; and then it would certainly be a strange thing if on the way of affliction there was the difference that there were some who walked on the way of affliction without afflictions. Thus the task is again established; the sufferer at once knows definitely what the task is, for the affliction is the way. If someone travels without afflictions, then so be it; then he merely goes on another road, which is his own affair. But doubt cannot lay hold on the sufferer and make him doubtful by the thought that others walk on the same way without afflictions. . . .

The affliction is the way — and this constitutes the joy: that it is consequently not a characteristic of the way, that it is hard, but a characteristic of the affliction, that it is the way, so the affliction must consequently lead to something, it must be something practicable and appreciable, not superhuman. . . .

Is this not joyful! How confidently the sufferer can breathe in this thought! He not only commits himself into the hands of God and goes to meet the affliction; no, he says: "The affliction itself is a sign to me that I am well advised, the affliction is my helper — for the affliction is the way." As long as the child still has a timid fear of the teacher, it can no doubt learn much; but when confidence has driven out the fear, and fearlessness has triumphed; then the higher instruction begins. And thus, too, when the sufferer, assured that the affliction is the way, has overcome the affliction; for is not this in the higher sense overcoming affliction, to be willing to believe that the affliction is the way, is the helper! The Apostle Paul says somewhere, "Faith is our victory," and in another place, "Yea, we are more than conquerors." But can one do more than conquer? Yes, if before the strife begins he has transformed the enemy into a friend. That is what it means to conquer in affliction, to overcome affliction, as one overcomes an enemy, assuming that the affliction is one's enemy. But it is more than conquering to believe that the affliction is one's friend, that it is not an obstacle on the way, but the way, not the hindering but the improving, not the discouraging but the ennobling. . . .

Wonderful! The way of affliction is the only one where there is no hindrance, for the affliction itself prepares the way instead of blocking it. But is not this good news! For what is more distressing than when a wayfarer must say: "Here there is no longer a path." And hence what is more joyful than that a wayfarer constantly dares say: "Here there is always a way!"

The Power of Love

The love which covers a multitude of sins is never deceived. When the heart is niggardly, when one gives with one eye and

THE MOMENT [1855]

with seven eyes looks to see what one will get in return, then one easily discovers a multitude of sins. But when the heart is filled with love, then the eye is never deceived; for love when it gives, does not scrutinize the gift, but its eyes are fixed on the Lord. When the heart is filled with envy, then the eye has power to call forth uncleanness even in the pure; but when love dwells in the heart, then the eye has power to foster the good in the unclean; but his eye does not see the evil but the pure, which it loves and encourages by loving it. Certainly there is a power in this world which by its words turns good into evil, but there is a power above which turns the evil into good; that power is the love which covers a multitude of sins. When hate dwells in the heart, then sin lies at a man's door, and its manifold desires exist in him; but when love dwells in the heart, then sin flees far away, and he sees it no more. When disputes, malice, wrath, quarrels, dissensions, factions fill the heart, does one then need to go far in order to discover the multitudinousness of sin, or does a man need to live very long to produce these outside of himself! But when joy, peace, longsuffering, gentleness, goodness, faith, meekness and temperance dwell in the heart, what wonder, then, that a man, even if he were surrounded by a multitude of sins, remains an alien, a stranger, who understands only a very little about the customs of the country, even if these were explained to him? Would not this, then, be a covering of the multitude of sins?

✥

The Task at Hand

Plato says somewhere in his Republic that things will go well only when those men shall govern the state who do not desire to govern. The idea is probably that, assuming the necessary capability, a man's reluctance to govern affords a good guarantee that he will govern well and efficiently; whereas a man desirous of governing may very easily either abuse his power and become a tyrant, or by his desire to govern be brought into an unforeseen situation of dependence on the people he is to rule, so that his government really becomes an illusion.

This observation applies also to other relations where much depends on taking things seriously: assuming there is ability in a man, it is best that he show reluctance to meddle with them. It is, to be sure, true as the proverb has it: "Where there is a will there is a way;" but true seriousness is seen only when a man fully equal to his task is forced, against his will, to undertake it — against his will, but fully equal to the task.

In this sense I may say of myself

111

that I bear a correct relation to the task at hand: to work in the present moment, for God knows that nothing is more distasteful to me.

Authorship — well, I confess that I find it pleasant; and I may as well admit that I have clearly loved to write — in the manner, to be sure, which suits me. And what I have loved to do is precisely the opposite of working in the present moment. What I have loved is precisely remoteness from the present moment — that remoteness in which, like a lover, I may dwell on my thoughts and, like an artist in love with his instrument, entertain myself with language and lure from it the expressions demanded by my thoughts — ah blissful passtime! In an eternity I should not weary of this occupation.

To contend with men — well, I do like it in a certain sense; for I have by nature a temperament so polemic that I feel in my element only when surrounded by men's mediocrity and meanness. But only on one condition, viz., that I be permitted to scorn them in silence and to satisfy the master passion of my soul: scorn — opportunity for which my career as an author has often enough given me.

I am therefore a man of whom it may be said truthfully that he is not in the least desirous to work in the present moment — very probably I have been called to do so for that very reason.

Now that I am to work in the present moment I must, alas! say farewell to thee, beloved remoteness, where there was no necessity to hurry, but always plenty of time, where I could wait for hours and days and weeks for the proper expression to occur to me, whereas now I must break with all such regards of tender love. And now that I am to work in the present moment I find that there will be not a few persons to whom I owe it to pay my respects to all the insignificant things which mediocrity with great self-importance will lecture about; to all the nonsense which mediocre people, by interpreting into my words their own mediocrity, will find in all I write; and to all the lies and calumnies to which a man is exposed against whom those two great powers in society, envy and stupidity, must of necessity conspire.

Why, then, do I wish to work in the present moment? Because I should forever repent of not having done so and forever repent of having been discouraged by the consideration that the generation now living would find a presentation of the essential truths of Christianity interesting and curious reading, at most; having accomplished which, they will calmly remain where they are, that is, in the illusion that they are Christians and that the clergy's playing with Christianity really is Christianity.

A Great Delusion

Every physician will admit that by the correct diagnosis of a malady more that half the fight against it is won; also that if a correct diagnosis has not been made, all skill and all care and attention will be of little avail.

The same is true with regard to religion.

All agreed to let stand the claim that in "Christendom" we are all Christians, every one of us; and then we have laid and, perhaps, will lay, emphasis now on this, now on that, side of the teachings of the Scriptures.

But the truth is: we are not only not Christians — no, we are not even the heathen to whom Christianity may be taught without misgivings, and what is worse, we are prevented through a delusion, an enormous delusion (viz. "Christendom," the Christian state, a Christian country, a Christian world) from becoming Christians.

And then the suggestion is made to one to continue untouched and unchanged this delusion and, rather, to furnish a new presentation of the teachings of Christ.

This has been suggested; and in a certain sense, it is altogether fitting. Just because one lives in a delusion (not to speak even of being interested in keeping up the delusion), one is bound to desire that which will feed the malady — a common enough observation this — the sick man desiring precisely those things which feed his malady.

When Christianity Becomes a Drug

What Christianity needs is not a stifling protection of the state — ah no, it needs fresh air, it needs persecution and — the protection of God. The state does only mischief in averting persecution and surely is not the medium through which God's protection can be conducted. Whatever you do, save Christianity from the state, for with its protection it overlies Christianity like a fat woman overlying her child with her carcass, besides teaching Christianity the most abominable bad habits — as, e.g., to use the police force and to call that Christianity. . . .

A person is growing thinner every day and is wasting away. What may the trouble be? For surely he is not suffering want! "No, sure enough," says the doctor, "that is not the trouble. The trouble is precisely with his eating, with his eating in season and out of season, with his eating without being hungry, with his using stimulants to produce an appetite, and in this manner ruining his digestion, so that he is wasting away as if he suffered want."

The same is true in religion. The worst of all is to satisfy a craving which has not as yet made its appearance, to anticipate it, or — worse still — by the help of stimulants to produce something which looks like a craving, which then is promptly satisfied. Ah, the shame of it! And yet this is exactly what is being done in religion where people are in very truth fooled out of the real meaning of life and helped to waste their lives.

That is in very truth the effect of this whole machinery of a state church and a thousand royal officials who, under the pretense of being spiritual guides for the people, trick them out of the highest thing in life, which is the solicitude about one's self and the need which would surely of itself find a teacher or minister after its own mind, whereas now the need — and it is just the growth of this sense of a need which gives life its highest significance — whereas now this need does not arise at all, but on the contrary is forestalled by being satisfied long before it can arise. And this is the way, they claim, this is the way to continue the work which the Savior of Mankind did begin — stunting the

By seeing the glorious ones, the witnesses to the truth, venture everything for Christianity, one is led to the conclusion: Christianity must be truth. By considering the priest one is led to the conclusion: Christianity is hardly the truth, but profit is the truth.

human race as they do. And why is this so? Because there happen to be a thousand and one royal officials who have to support their families by furnishing what is called — spiritual guidance for men's souls!

Christendom is a Fraud

There is only one relation to revealed truth: believing it.

The fact that one believes can be proved in only one way: by being willing to suffer for one's faith. And the degree of one's faith is proved only by the degree of one's willingness to suffer for one's faith.

In that way Christianity came into the world, being served by witnesses who were willing absolutely to suffer everything for their faith, and who actually had to suffer, to sacrifice life and blood for the truth.

The courage of their faith makes an impression upon the human race, leading it to the following conclusion: What is able thus to inspire men to sacrifice everything, to venture life and blood, must be truth.

This is the proof which is adduced for the truth of Christianity.

Now, on the contrary, the priest is so kind as to wish to make it a livelihood. But a livelihhood is exactly the opposite of suffering, of being sacrificed, in which the proof consists: it is the opposite of proving the truth of Christianity by the fact that there have lived men who have sacrificed everything, ventured life and blood for Christianity.

Here then is the proof and the disproof at the same time! The proof of the truth of Christianity from the fact that one has ventured everything for it, is disproved, or rendered suspect, by the fact that the priest who advances this proof does exactly the opposite. By seeing the glorious ones, the witnesses to the truth, venture everything for Christianity, one is led to the conclusion: Christianity must be truth. By considering the priest one is led to the conclusion: Christianity is hardly the truth, but profit is the truth.

No, the proof that something is truth from the willingness to suffer for it can only be advanced by one who himself is willing to suffer for it. The priest's proof — proving the truth of Christianity by the fact that he takes money for it, profits by, lives off it, being steadily promoted, with a family, lives off of the fact that others have suffered — is a self-contradiction; Christianly regarded, it is fraud.

And therefore, Christianly, the priest must be stopped — in the sense in which one speaks of stopping a thief. And as people cry, "Hip, ho!" after a Jew, so, until no priest is any more to be seen, they must cry, "Stop thief! Stop him, he is stealing what belongs to the glorious ones!" What they deserved by their noble disinterestedness, and what they did not get, being rewarded by unthankfulness, persecuted and put to death, that the priest steals by appropriating their lives, by describing their sufferings, proving the truth of Christianity by the willingness of these glorious ones to suffer for it. Thus it is the priest robs the glorious ones; and then he deceives the simple-minded human multitude, which has not the ability to see through the priest's traffic and perceive that he proves

THE MOMENT [1855]

the truth of Christianity and at the same time disproves it.

What wonder, then, that Christianity simply does not exist, that the notion of "Christendom" is galimatias, when those who are Christians are such in reliance upon the priest's proof, and assume that Christianity is truth in reliance upon the priest's proof: that something is truth because one is willing enough to make profit out of it, or perhaps even (by a greater refinement) to get the extra profit of protesting that he is willing to suffer. To assume the truth of Christianity in reliance upon this proof is just as nonsensical as to regard oneself as an opulent man because much money passes through one's hands which is not one's own, or because one possesses a lot of paper money issued by a bank which is insolvent.

An Eternity to Repent in

Once upon a time there lived somewhere in the East a poor old couple. Utterly poor they were, and anxiety about the future naturally grew when they thought of old age approaching. They did not, indeed, constantly assail heaven with their prayers; they were too God-fearing to do that; but still they were ever praying to God for help.

Then one morning it happened that the old woman found an exceeding large jewel on the hearthstone, which she forthwith showed to her husband, who recognized its value and easily perceived that now their poverty was at an end.

What a bright future for these old people, and what gladness! But frugal and pious as they were they decided not to sell the jewel just yet, since they had enough wherewithal to live for a while yet. But on the morrow they would sell it, and then a new life was to begin for them.

In the following night the woman dreamed that she was transported to Paradise. An angel showed her about in the splendors which an Oriental imagination can devise. He showed her a hall in which there stood long rows of armchairs gemmed all over with precious stones and pearls. These, so the angel explained, were the seats of the pious. And last of all he pointed out to her the one destined for herself. When regarding it more closely she discovered that a very large jewel was lacking in the back of the chair, and she asked the angel how that might be. . . .

The angel answered: "That was the jewel which you found on your hearthstone. It was given you ahead of time, and it cannot be put in again."

In the morning the woman told her husband this dream. And she was of the opinion that it was better, perhaps, to endure

116

in poverty the few years still left to them to live, rather than to be without that jewel in all eternity. And her pious husband was of the same opinion.

So in the evening they laid the jewel on the hearthstone and prayed to God to make it away again. And next morning it had disappeared, for certain; and what had become of it the old folks well knew: it was in its right place again. . . .

Heed this well! You may by worldly wisdom escape perhaps what it has pleased God to unite with the condition of one's being a Christian, that is, sufferings and tribulations; you may, and to your own destruction, by cleverly avoiding the difficulties, perhaps, gain what God has forever made incompatible with being a Christian, that is, the enjoyment of pleasures and all earthly goods; you may, fooled by your own worldly wisdom, perhaps, finally perish altogether, in the illusion that you are on the right road because you have gained happiness in this world: and then — you will have an eternity to repent in! An eternity to repent in; to repent that you did not employ your time in doing what might be remembered in all eternity; that is, in truth to love God, with the consequence that you suffer the persecution of men in this life.

Therefore, do not deceive yourself, and of all deceivers fear most yourself! Even if it were possible for one, with regard to eternity, to have something in advance, you would still deceive yourself just by having something in advance of time - and then an eternity to repent in! ∎

"God, let me never forget that even if I did not win a single person — if my life expresses that I fear You, then all is won. On the other hand, if I won all people — if my life does not express that I fear You, then all is lost."

Journals 1851

1797 *April 4* Michael Pedersen Kierkegaard marries Ane Sørensdatter Lund.
July 7 Birth of their first child.
1813 *May 5* Søren Aabye Kierkegaard is born.
1821 Enrolled in Borgerdydsskolen, Copenhagen.
1830 *Oct. 30* Begins theological studies at University of Copenhagen.
1834 Mother dies. First journal entry.
1837 *May 9* Meets Regine Olsen. Moves away from home. Begins teaching Latin at Borgerdydsskolen.
1838 *May 19* The "indescribable joy" journal entry.
Aug. 8 Father dies. The "great earthquake".
Sept. 7 Publishes *From the Papers of One Still Living* (a critique of Hans Christian Andersen's latest novel, *Only a Fiddler*).
1840 *July 3* Completes final theological exam (magna cum laude).
July 19 Journey to Sædding. Returns August 6.
Sept. 8 Proposes to Regine Olsen. Two days later the engagement is announced.
1841 *Jan. 12* Preaches sermon at Holmens Church.
Aug. 11 Returns engagement ring to Regine.
Sept. 29 Defends dissertation for master's degree (later called doctoral degree), *The Concept of Irony, with constant reference to Socrates*.
Oct. 11 Final break with Regine.
Oct. 25 Travels to Berlin to attend Schelling's lectures. Returns March 6, 1842.
1843 *Feb. 20* Publishes *Either/Or: A Fragment of Life*, edited by Victor Eremita.
May 8 Second visit to Berlin.
May 16 Publishes *Two Edifying Discourses*, by S. Kierkegaard.
July Regine becomes engaged to Fridrich Schlegel.
Oct. 16 Publishes *Repetition: An attempt at experimental Psychology*, by Constantin Constantius; *Fear and Trembling: Dialectic Lyrics*, by Johannes de Silentio; and *Three Edifying Discourses*, by S. Kierkegaard.
Dec. 6 Publishes *Four Edifying Discourses*, by S. Kierkegaard.
1844 *Feb. 24* Preaches sermon at Trinitatis Church.
March 5 Publishes *Two Edifying Discourses*, by S. Kierkegaard.
June 8 Publishes *Three Edifying Discourses*, by S. Kierkegaard.
June 13 Publishes *Philosophical Fragments*, by Johannes Climacus.
June 17 Publishes *The Concept of Dread*, by Vigilius Haufniensis; and *Prefaces*, by Nicholaus Notabene.
Aug. 31 Publishes *Four Edifying Discourses*, by S. Kierkegaard.
1845 *April 29* Publishes *Three Discourses on Imagined Occasions*, by S. Kierkegaard.
April 30 Publishes *Stages on Life's Way*, edited by Hilarius Bookbinder.
May 13 Third visit to Berlin. Returns May 24.
May 29 Publishes *Eighteen Edifying Discourses*, by S. Kierkegaard.
Dec. 27 In an article in the paper *Fædrelandet*, Frater Taciturnus challenges *The Corsair* to write about him.
1846 *Jan. 2* *The Corsair* starts attacking Kierkegaard.
Feb. 7 Considers terminating his writing career and becoming a minister.
Feb. 27 Publishes *Concluding Unscientific Postscript to the "Philosophical Fragments"*,

by Johannes Climacus.
March 30 Publishes *A Literary Review* (including "The Present Age"), by S. Kierkegaard.
May 2 Fourth visit to Berlin. Returns May 16. Studies A.P. Adler's books on Christianity.
1847 *March 13* Publishes *Edifying Discourses in Various Spirits*, by S. Kierkegaard.
Sept. 29 Publishes *Works of Love*, by S. Kierkegaard.
Nov. 3 Regine married to Fridrich Schlegel.
Dec. 24 Sells childhood home on Nytorv.
1848 *April 19* Spiritual breakthrough.
April 26 Publishes *Christian Discourses*, by S. Kierkegaard.
Aug. Journal entry about poor health and death approaching.
Sept. 1 Preaches sermon at Our Lady's cathedral.
Nov. Finishes *The Point of View for my Work as an Author* (published posthumously in 1859).
1849 *Feb.* The idea of becoming a martyr for Christ begins to take shape.
May 19 Publishes *Two Minor Ethical-Religious Treatises*, by H. H.
July 30 Publishes *The Sickness unto Death: A Christian-psychological exposition for edification and awakening*, by Anti-Climacus.
Nov. 13 Publishes *Three Discourses at the Communion on Fridays* (including "The Highpriest," "The Publican," and "The Woman Taken in Sin"), by S. Kierkegaard.
1850 *Sept. 27* Publishes *Training in Christianity*, by Anti-Climacus.
Dec. 20 Publishes *An Edifying Discourse*, by S. Kierkegaard.

Aug. 7 Publishes *On My Work as an Author*; and *Two Discourses at Holy Communion on Fridays*, by S. Kierkegaard.
Sept. 10 Publishes *For Self-Examination, Recommended to the Contemporary Age*, by S. Kierkegaard.
1851-52 Writes *Judge for Yourself* (published posthumously in 1876).
1854 *Jan. 30* Bishop Mynster dies.
April 15 Martensen appointed bishop.
Dec. 18 Publishes the first of 21 polemic articles in *Fædrelandet*.
1855 *May 24* Publishes the first issue of *The Moment*.
June 16 Publishes *Christ's Judgment on Official Christianity*, by S. Kierkegaard.
Sept. 3 Publishes *The Unchangeableness of God*, by S. Kierkegaard.
Sept. 25 Publishes the ninth issue of *The Moment* (number 10 published posthumously). Last journal entry.
Oct. 2 Hospitalized at Frederiksberg Hospital.
Nov. 11 Dies in the hospital and is buried a week later at Assistents Cemetery. ∎

119

BIBLIOGRAPHY

Villads Christensen, *Søren Kierkegaards vej til kristendommen*
(Munksgaard, Copenhagen, 1955)

Arild Christensen, *Kierkegaard og naturen*
(Graabrødre Torvs Antikvariat, Copenhagen, 1964)

Svend Leopold, *Søren Kierkegaard: Geniets tragedie*
(Gyldendalske Boghandel/Nordisk Forlag, Copenhagen 1932)

The Diary of Søren Kierkegaard,
Edited by Peter P. Rohde (Carol Publishing Group, New York, 1993)

Selections from the Writings of Kierkegaard, Edited and translated by Lee M. Hollander
(Doubleday & Company, Inc., New York, 1960)

Kenneth Hamilton, *The Promise of Kierkegaard*
(Lippincott Company, New York, 1969)

James Collins, *The Mind of Kierkegaard*
(Henry Regnery Company, Chicago, 1965)

Perry D. LeFevre, *The Prayers of Kierkegaard*
(The University of Chicago Press, Chicago, 1956)

Kierkegaard's Writings
(Princeton University Press, Princeton, 1978—)

Kierkegaard's Journals and Papers
(Indiana University Press, Bloomington, 1967–78)

Philosophy is perfectly right in saying that life must be understood backward. But then one forgets the other clause — that it must be lived forward.

To risk is to lose one's foothold for a while. Not to risk is to lose oneself forever.

Most men are subjective toward themselves and objective toward all others, frightfully objective sometimes — but the task is precisely to be objective toward oneself and subjective toward all others.

Everyone in whom the animal disposition is preponderant believes firmly that millions are more than one; whereas spirit is just the opposite, that one is more than millions, and that every man can be the one.

The objective problem consists of an inquiry into the truth of Christianity. The subjective problem concerns the relationship of the individual to Christianity.

To: Rocco and Sophie

Always remember Jesus is your Good Shepherd and He will lead you down the right Paths.

Paige Cartledge

GOD OPENED THE GATE FOR ME

A GO-TO PORTABLE PRAYER ROOM BY VICTORIA BRESCHAN

God Bless you
—Madysen Holecen

Copyright © 2015 Victoria Breschan.

Book design by: Cliff Muncy, MuncyWeb Design & Unique Marketing.
Editing by: Sara Muncy, Pattie Turner, and Linda Johnson.
Author photograph by: Sara Muncy Photography.
All other photographs © 2014 Mady Holder. Used by permission.

All rights reserved. No part of this book may be used or reproduced by any means, graphic, electronic, or mechanical, including photocopying, recording, taping or by any information storage retrieval system without the written permission of the publisher except in the case of brief quotations embodied in critical articles and reviews.

WestBow Press books may be ordered through booksellers or by contacting:

WestBow Press
A Division of Thomas Nelson & Zondervan
1663 Liberty Drive
Bloomington, IN 47403
www.westbowpress.com
1 (866) 928-1240

Because of the dynamic nature of the Internet, any web addresses or links contained in this book may have changed since publication and may no longer be valid. The views expressed in this work are solely those of the author and do not necessarily reflect the views of the publisher, and the publisher hereby disclaims any responsibility for them.

Scripture taken from the New Century Version®. Copyright © 2005 by Thomas Nelson. Used by permission.

ISBN: 978-1-4908-6586-7 (sc)
ISBN: 978-1-4908-6585-0 (e)

Library of Congress Control Number: 2015900256

Print information available on the last page.

WestBow Press rev. date: 3/30/2015

Dedicated in memory of

Orby (my Pa)
and
Mary (my Grandma)

In their lives, I witnessed the Peace that only God's Word can give.

Nanny

*The memories we made were full of unlimited
Grace, Love and Mercy. I love you Nanny!*

ACKNOWLEDGMENTS

Thanks to my husband. The man who loves me like God loves me: the good, the bad, and the ugly. He loves me in spite of my faults. He doesn't try to change the person God created me to be, but is not afraid to argue when necessary, and knows how to say "no" in a loving way. No matter what hair-brained idea I come up with, that I feel God is leading me to do, he is by my side to support me. For me, he is my perfect match, hand-picked by God. I love you more.

A special thank you to my Lord and Savior, Jesus Christ.

Thanks to Mady Holder; God has blessed your eyes to behold His Creation, and that special gift shines in the photography of this book.

Thanks to Cliff and Sara Muncy, Pattie Turner, and Linda Johnson. They know how to edit my rough edges.

TO: Gary

PREFACE

Have you ever met someone who just has a way of making everyone else around them feel calm? A person who is a joy to be around, and rock solid spiritually? Emerson was one of those people. Emerson was a co-worker of mine, and we worked in the emergency room together. He was a great nurse, and I loved when he was in charge. His calm, collected presence made everyone else relax. He was not only grounded in his professional life, but in his spiritual life as well. When he received a diagnosis of a disease that was associated with a grim prognosis, it was immediately evident that Christ was his anchor.

As an outreach project for the youth group at our church, I helped them put together a collection of encouraging Bible verses and devotions for Emerson. The idea was to give him something tangible that he could take to doctor visits and chemotherapy treatments, which might help him focus on his power source, Jesus, instead of becoming overwhelmed by the difficult journey ahead. Emerson has since gone to be with Jesus, but during those dark moments, he expressed that the little scrapbook of encouragement meant a lot to him.

OUR STORY

Words of

Encouragement

ADVENTURE

you're my No. 1

TO: Gary

It's what spurred on the concept for *God Opened The Gate For Me*, and it is my prayer that this little book will be of similar encouragement to you, no matter what you're going through.

In putting this devotional together, I am completely out of my comfort zone. It's totally a step of obedience for me. I am not a famous writer, or a grand public speaker. I am simply a nurse by trade, and a follower of Christ by choice. That choice to follow Christ was one of the best choices I have ever made. At the point of commitment when I said, "I promise it ALL to Him", I put all my chips on the table, and went all in. And so, here I am, stepping out of my comfort zone, and walking in obedience; all the while I'm praying that as you read this book you will have spiritual eyes to see the goodness of God, and spiritual ears to hear the sweet whispers of God's promises to you through His Word.

Victoria Bruschan

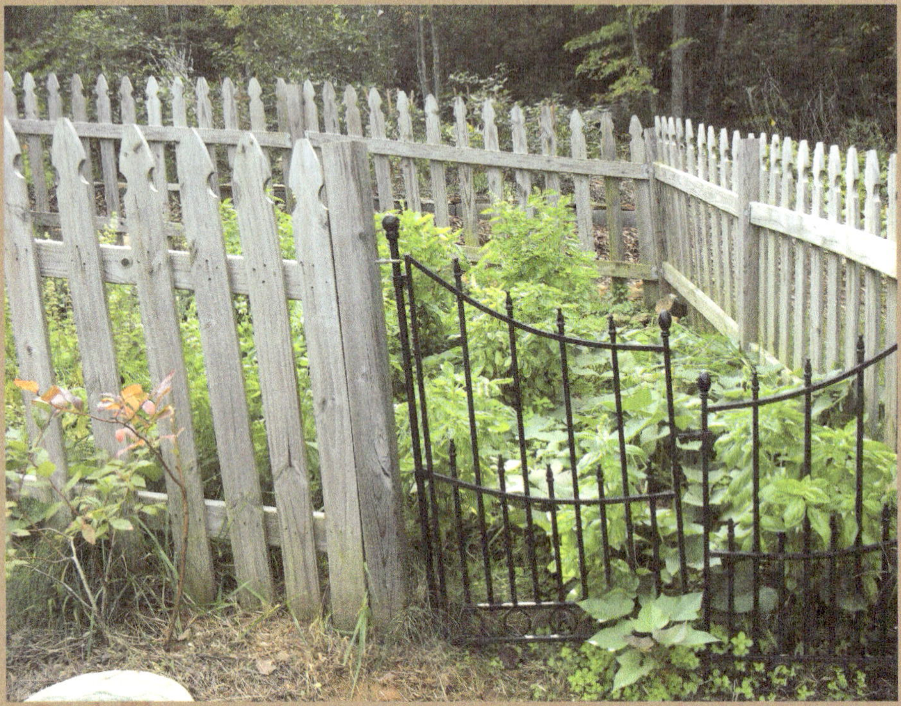

INTRODUCTION

This book contains a collection of Bible verses from my own spiritual journey, as well as verses and stories contributed by my close-knit group of prayer warriors. I have personally traveled many difficult paths, and have been through tough times, but it's in those times that I have been a witness to the power of God's Word, and the power of God's praying people. The praying people in my life are the glue that have held me together, and they remind me to look up to the Lord for peace. Peace that passes all understanding.

Instead of limiting the individual devotionals to a specific category that they might apply to, I decided it best to leave that up to the work of the Holy Spirit. Because who is to say that Psalm 121:1-2 wouldn't minister to someone drowning in debt as much as it would to a soldier fighting overseas? This book is designed to meet folks right where they are, and point them to spiritual rescue.

It is my hope that when you find yourself waist-deep in a difficult situation that seems too hard to bear, you can pull this book out, and find peace in God's Word. And, that your spirit will be rejuvenated, and refocused on what really matters.

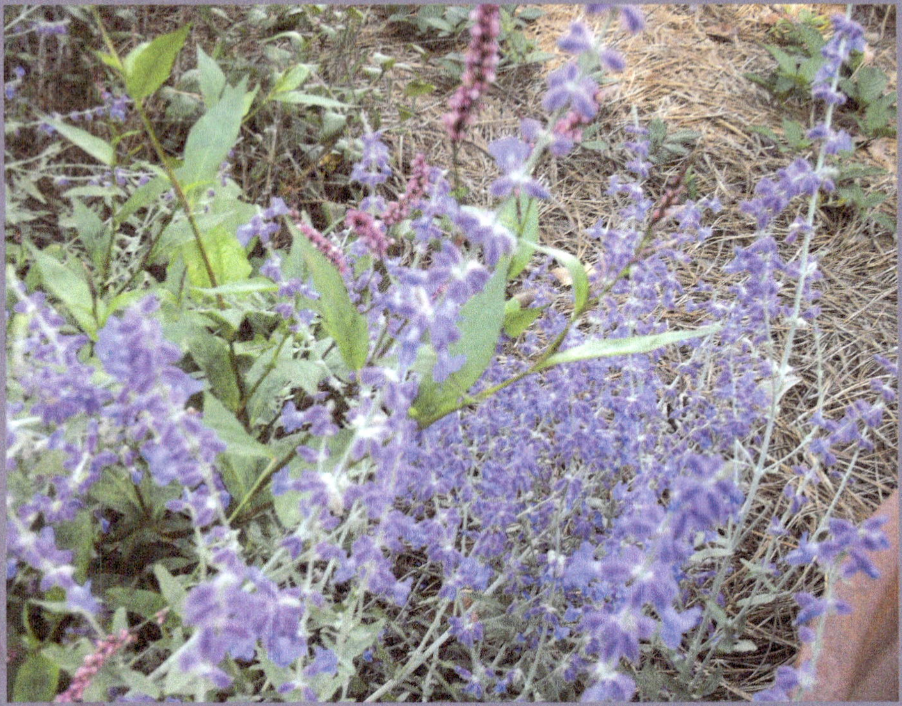

HELP

Psalm 121:1-2
I look to the hills,
but where does my help come from?
My help comes from the Lord,
who made heaven and earth.

I adopted this as my life verse from my Grandfather, who I called Pa. While putting together care packages for our troops during the Iraq War in 2003, Pa chose Psalm 121:1-2 as the scripture to encourage war torn and weary soldiers fighting overseas.

Psalm 23
The Lord is my shepherd;
I have everything I need.
He lets me rest in green pastures.
He leads me to calm water.
He gives me new strength.
He leads me on paths that are right
for the good of his name.
Even if I walk through a very dark valley,
I will not be afraid,
because you are with me.
Your rod and your shepherd's staff comfort me.
You prepare a meal for me
in front of my enemies.
You pour oil of blessing on my head;
you fill my cup to overflowing.
Surely your goodness and love will be with me
all my life,
and I will live in the house of the Lord forever.

"Always remember that Jesus is your Good Shepherd, and He knows your name, and He will lead you in the right paths beside the still waters. I love you, and I am proud of you."

When I was ten years old, my Sunday School teacher gave me a devotional book, and jotted the words of encouragement quoted above on the inside cover. Little did we know, after traveling across the United States and overseas with the devotional, those words would be the very thing that the Holy Spirit used to lead me back to Christ 25 years later.

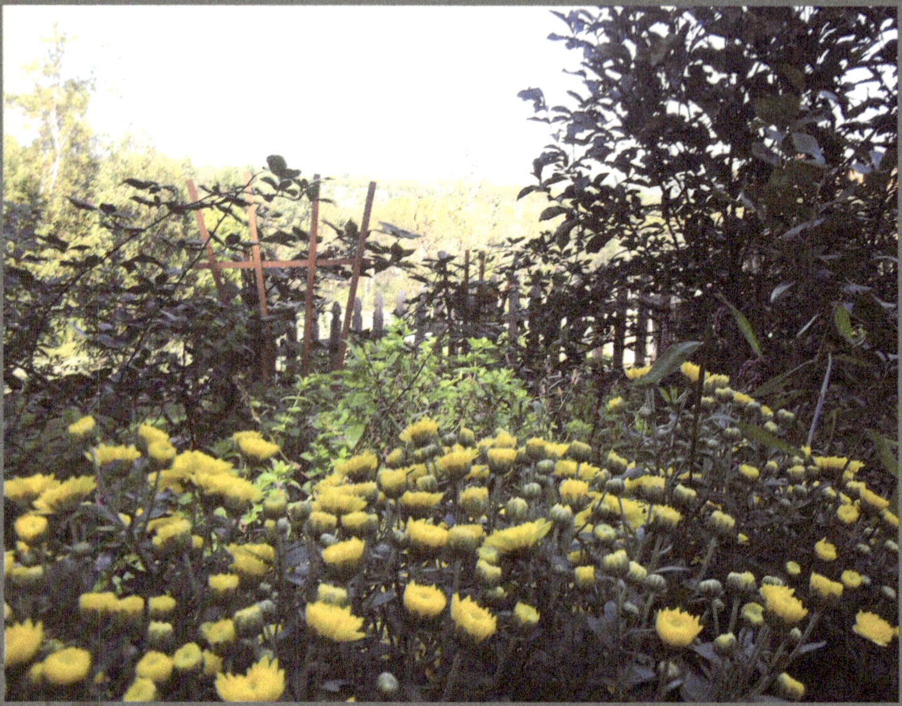

OUR PROTECTION

Psalm 91:9-12
The Lord is your protection;
you have made God Most High your place of safety.
Nothing bad will happen to you;
no disaster will come to your home.
He has put his angels in charge of you
to watch over you wherever you go.
They will catch you in their hands
so that you will not hit your foot on a rock.

The entire chapter of Psalm 91 is very special to my mother. She reads it because it gives her strength. This Psalm speaks about God's protection over His children, and so it is fitting that my mother began reading these verses once a week after we found out my father had a tumor. His doctor told us that he suspected it was cancer, and gave him only six months to live. Thankfully the doctor was wrong about my father's prognosis. Over ten years later, my father is still with us today, alive and well!

My parents have been married for forty-nine years, and my mother continues to read those protection verses every week, and she prompts me to do the same. My favorite verses in this chapter are 14-16, which not only reinforce the promise of God's protection, but also the promise of His presence in times of trouble, and the mighty rescuing power of the Holy Spirit which testifies of God's salvation:

Psalm 91:14-16
The Lord says, "Whoever loves me, I will save.
I will protect those who know me.
They will call to me, and I will answer them.
I will be with them in trouble;
I will rescue them and honor them.
I will give them a long, full life,
and they will see how I can save."

*Thanks, Mom and Dad, for introducing me
to my best friend, Jesus.*

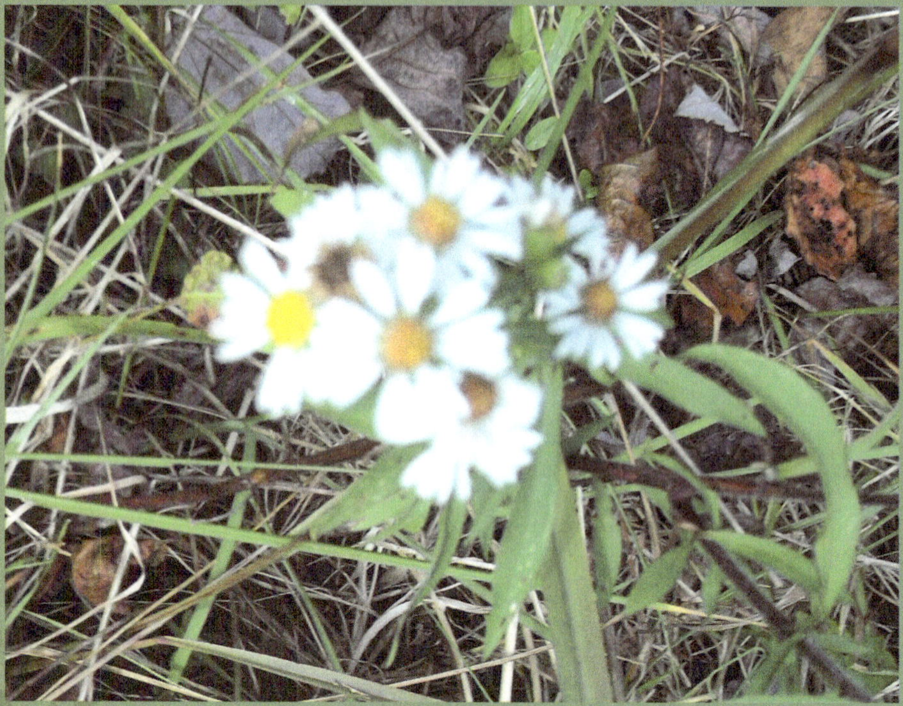

RUTH

John 14:2-3
There are many rooms in my Father's house; I would not tell you this if it were not true. I am going there to prepare a place for you. After I go and prepare a place for you, I will come back and take you to be with me so that you may be where I am.

2 Corinthians 5:7
We live by what we believe, not by what we can see.

Some days are more stressful than others.

My co-worker and fellow prayer warrior, Ruth, shared these verses which can help refocus our spirit when it seems like injustice prevails, and we struggle to keep our "Christ Face" on. When we focus our hearts and minds on the matters of eternity, temporary earthly things that we see happening around us become small and dim.

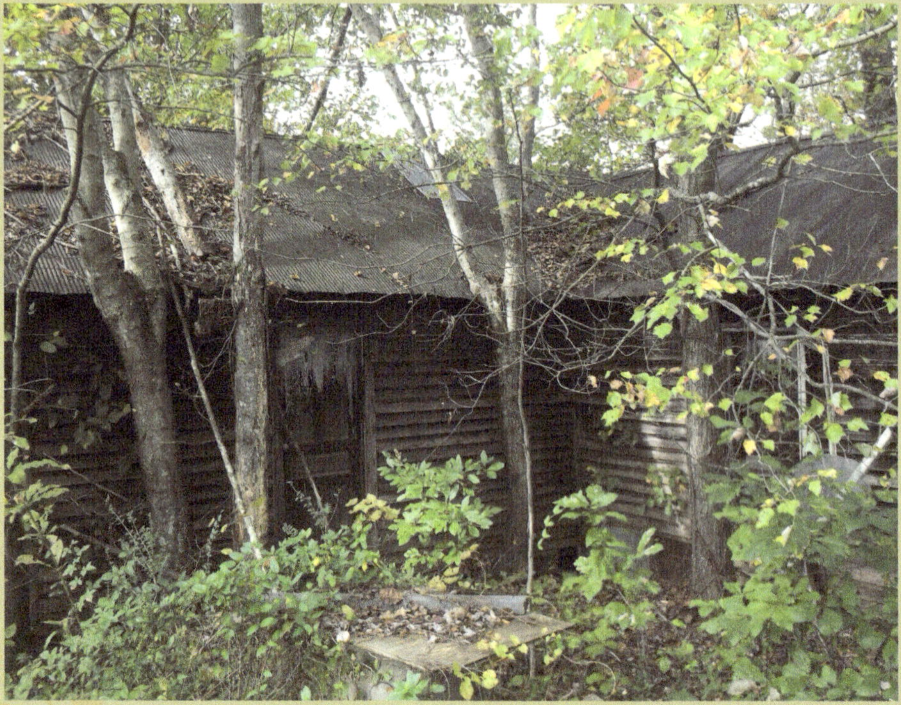

MIRIAM

Psalm 1:1-3
Happy are those who don't listen to the wicked,
who don't go where sinners go,
who don't do what evil people do.
They love the Lord's teachings,
and they think about those teachings day and night.
They are strong, like a tree planted by a river.
The tree produces fruit in season,
and its leaves don't die.
Everything they do will succeed.

These are some of Miriam's favorite verses. The number of people that share Miriam's hope of being with the Lord one day in His house amazes me. She says that hope in this sustains her on rough days at work. Earth is not her home. She's only passing through.

Jeremiah 29:11
"I say this because I know what I am planning for you,"
says the Lord. "I have good plans for you, not plans to
hurt you. I will give you hope and a good future."

Miriam is a great prayer warrior. She is in God's Word often, and more importantly she clings to it in times of trouble. Just in the past two years she has suffered the loss of both her mother and her husband, who are now with the Lord. I've heard her say it would be so great to be with them in Heaven.

"I'm ready Lord".

It's in the moments when despair and loneliness creep in, that she can cling to this verse, and be given hope that the Lord's plans are good, and He has a good future planned for her as His child.

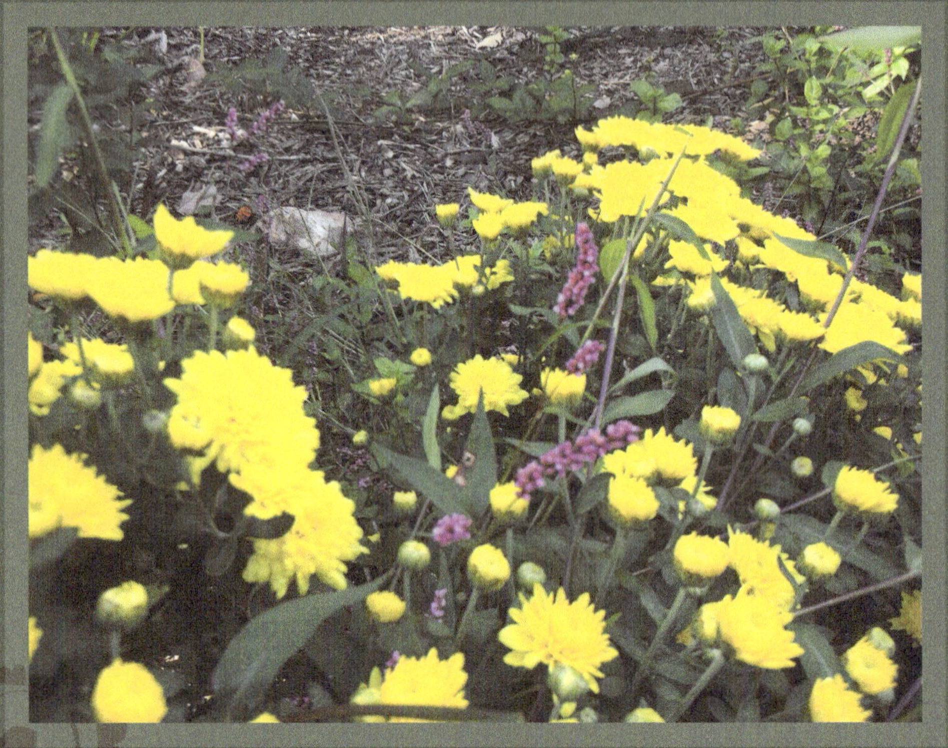

ELIZABETH

Joel 2:25
"Though I sent my great army against you—
those swarming locusts and hopping locusts,
the destroying locusts and the cutting locusts that ate your crops—
I will pay you back
for those years of trouble."

2 Timothy 2:25-26
"The Lord's servant must gently teach those who disagree. Then maybe God will let them change their minds so they can accept the truth. And they may wake up and escape from the trap of the devil, who catches them to do what he wants."

Elizabeth is one of my guardian angels.

For nine years Elizabeth prayed for me as if I were her child. She knew I was far from God, but that did not hinder her. Many years later we reconnected, and her prayers were answered: I had returned to God. The timing of our reconnection was nothing short of miraculous.

Shortly after our reunion, she lost her daughter at the of age 49. She began caring for her grandchildren, and was faced with what she described as a locust, one that was eating away at one of her grandchildren, John. By God's grace, He had prepared me to return a blessing, and help her during this trying time. Elizabeth, and her husband Zacharias, took their troubled grandchild into their home and began a Christian based rehab program.

In Elizabeth's own words, she says "I am asking the Lord to restore unto John the years the locusts have eaten up. I also pray for the Lord to give beauty for his ashes." Zacharias' verse that he has claimed and devoted to John's recovery is Isaiah 61:3, which says:

"I will give them a crown to replace their ashes,
and the oil of gladness to replace their sorrow,
and clothes of praise to replace their spirit of sadness.
Then they will be called Trees of Goodness,
trees planted by the Lord to show his greatness."

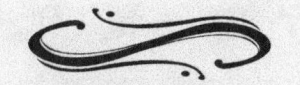

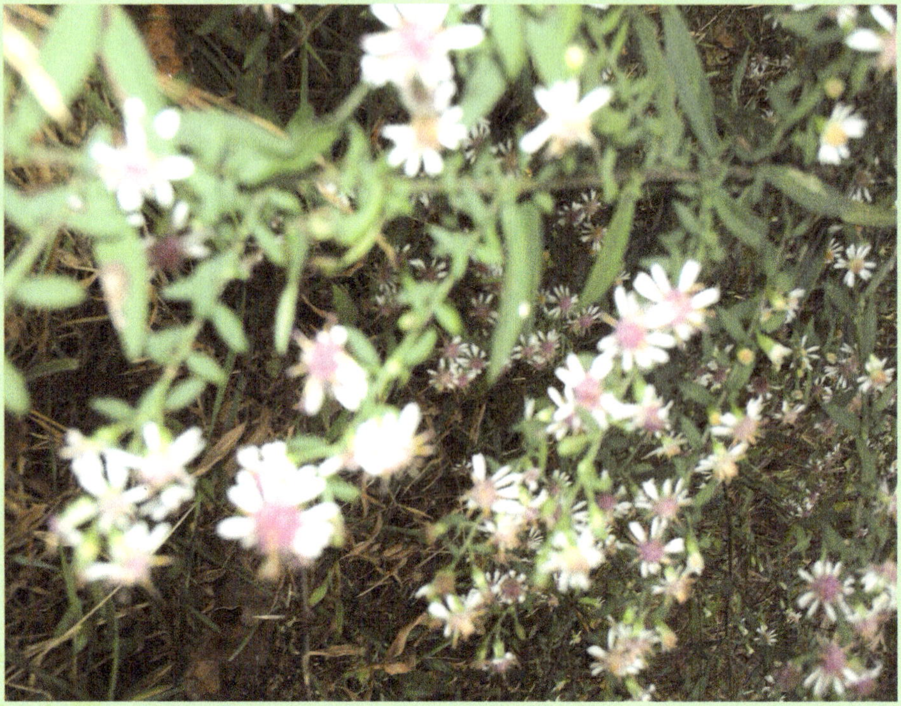

ESTHER

Esther is my daughter in Christ who has faced many trials and hardships over the years, but by God's grace, overcomes. I was interviewed not long ago for a management position, and a panel of four people asking a series of questions conducted the interview. One of the questions was what I considered to be my greatest accomplishment. My answer was, simply, Esther. Esther is a young lady that had an addiction for many years. When I first met her, I was working with her dad, and he told me his daughter was returning home after being in a Christian based rehab, and he asked me to be her accountability partner.

I said no. **God** had other plans.

While driving to work the next morning I was listening to a local Christian radio station, and I heard a man preaching on Romans 12. He asked the audience if we were Romans 12 Christians. Sure, we may think we're being good Christians because we go to church, or teach Sunday School, but have we taken the time to invest and pour our lives into another one of God's creations?

That day, that moment, I experienced a "burning bush". It wasn't an easy adventure, but it was, and is, one of the most believing seasons of my life. One of the things I enjoy most in my spiritual journey on this earth is when a "God thing" happens. These are times or experiences when you feel like God traveled from Heaven just to wrap his arms around you, and give you a big hug. There have been many of these times with Esther. Pouring my life into Esther's, and hers into mine, have been some of the happiest times for me. I am so proud of her. Esther has fully recovered, and has become a great warrior for God's army.

I am blessed and honored to be a part of God's plan for her life. The following pages recount Esther's story and testimony in her own words, and are accompanied by specific scriptures which have been so important to her spiritual journey.

ESTHER: HER WORDS, HER JOURNEY

Jeremiah 29:11
"I say this because I know what I am planning for you," says the Lord. "I have good plans for you, not plans to hurt you. I will give you hope and a good future."

This is a favorite of mine for all areas of life. During addiction recovery it was crucial for me to remember that no matter what had happened in my past, or how bleak my life had become, or how little I had left in life, God had a real plan for my future. That plan that included prospering and serving His kingdom, but most importantly, that promise of His plan gave me hope.

Isaiah 43:1-3
Now this is what the Lord says.
He created you, people of Jacob;
he formed you, people of Israel.
He says, "Don't be afraid, because I have saved you.
I have called you by name, and you are mine.
When you pass through the waters, I will be with you.
When you cross rivers, you will not drown.
When you walk through fire, you will not be burned,
nor will the flames hurt you.
This is because I, the Lord, am your God,
the Holy One of Israel, your Savior.
I gave Egypt to pay for you,
and I gave Cush and Seba to make you mine."

These scriptures from Isaiah helped me through my recovery, and also through difficult moments while my husband, James, was serving in the military overseas in Korea. It's giving me hope and comfort even now as we gear up for him to spend twelve months in Afghanistan in the Kandahar province, one of the most dangerous areas in that country.

I know God will always walk with me. His right hand will guide me, and even when I am barely treading water, or when the river swells, and I feel like I'm going to be overtaken, He promises that the waters will not overtake me, nor will the fires consume me.

God never promises that hard times won't happen, but in this scripture, and in so many others, He promises that He will not let us be defeated.

Philippians 4:8
Brothers and sisters, think about the things that are good and worthy of praise. Think about the things that are true and honorable and right and pure and beautiful and respected.

During my many years as a single mother, even after being set free from addiction, depression, anxiety, fear, and worthlessness, I still struggled to see how minimum wage jobs could ever turn into a bright and prosperous future. I was going to school full-time, working part-time, and could only afford to live in my parents' house, which was not the best environment. During that time, I constantly meditated on this verse as a reminder to cling to God's Word and His promises.

*He promised me in Jeremiah 29:11 that I **would** prosper, and I **would** have hope for the future.*

*He promised in Isaiah 43 that I **would not** be overtaken or consumed by trials.*

Philippians 4:8 helped bring my focus back to those promises.

All of these scriptures helped me take life one day at a time, and to remember what was true about myself, my future, and my relationship with God.

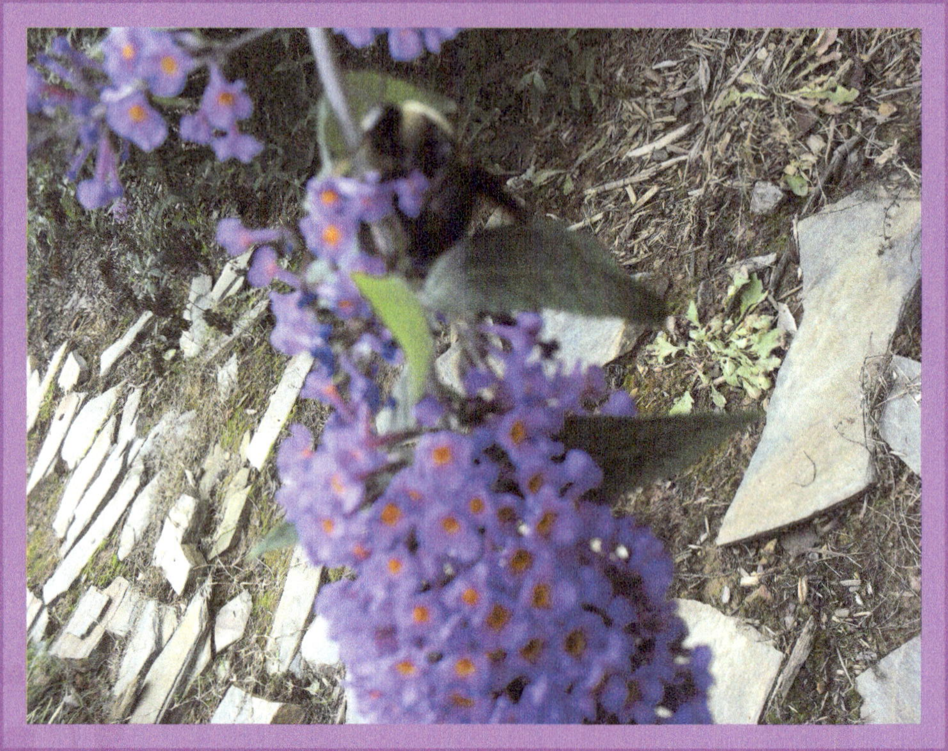

SAMUEL

Psalm 113:9
*He gives children to the woman who has none
and makes her a happy mother.
Praise the Lord!*

This is Samuel's life verse, because this is his real life story.

Psalm 113:9 was given to him by the mother Christ chose for him, not his biological mother. Samuel was a foster baby. If you don't believe God has a plan for each of His children, you should spend some time talking to Samuel's new mommy. She and her husband had become foster parents after losing a little boy at birth.

Their first foster experience was horrific and they contemplated never doing it again, and questioned whether this was God's plan for them. Then an unexpected sequence of events initiated by a complete stranger turned things around. After God's symphony began to play, it became a beautiful collection of miracle after miracle. It was clear it was orchestrated by the hand of God to fulfill His plan for a loving couple, and a little baby boy that needed a lot of love.

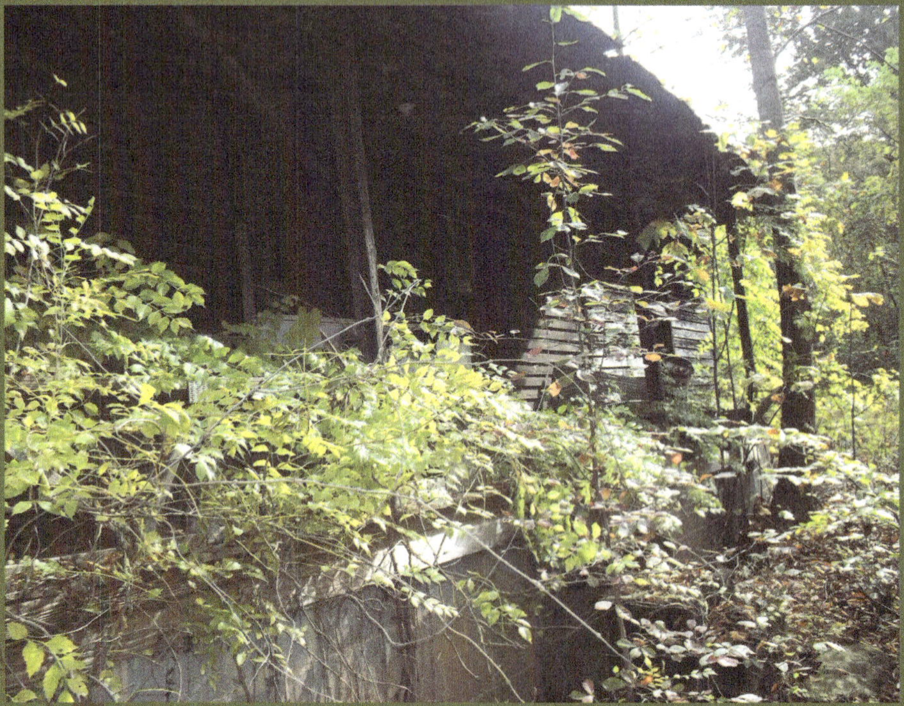

MARY

Psalm 68:5
God is in his holy Temple.
He is a father to orphans,
and he defends the widows.

When God made Mary, I think He had me in mind all along. She has been my friend since high school. Being my friend hasn't always been easy, but if anyone could do it, Mary could. She is one of the strongest Christian women I know, with a rock solid relationship with God that has been put through the fire. At a young age, her husband died, leaving her with two young girls to raise. Where so many would have turned their back on God, she clung to His hand.

God promises in Psalm 68:5 to be a father to the orphan, and a defender of the widow. That promise is one that Mary rested upon, and it gave her the strength to trust God even in the presence of profound grief.

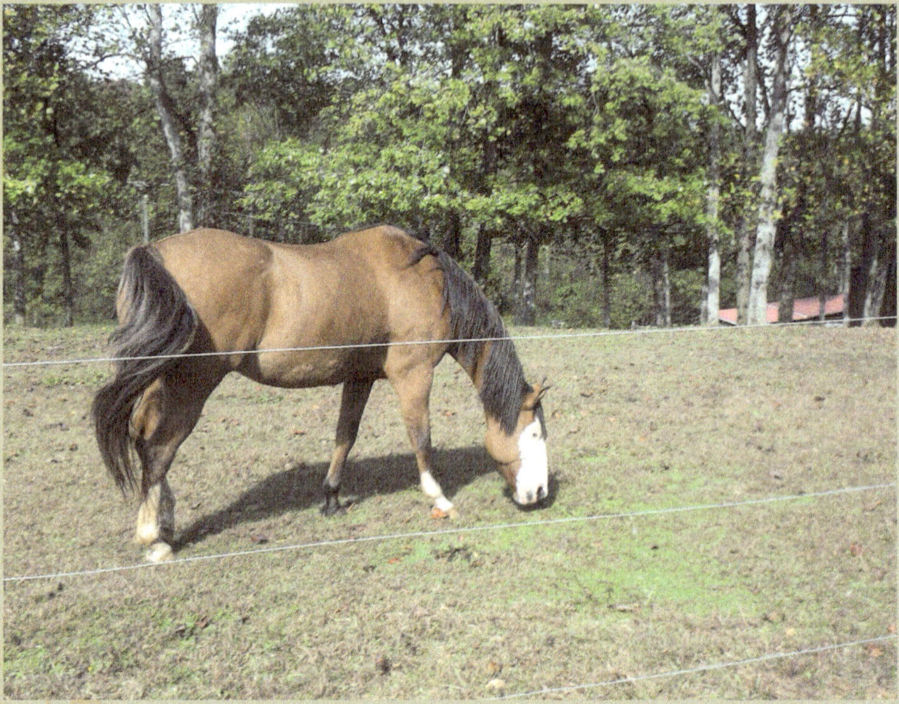

HANNAH

Joshua 1:9
*"Remember that I commanded you to be strong
and brave. Don't be afraid, because the Lord your
God will be with you everywhere you go."*

Ephesians 4:1-6
*I am in prison because I belong to the Lord. Therefore I urge
you who have been chosen by God to live up to the life to
which God called you. Always be humble, gentle, and patient,
accepting each other in love. You are joined together with
peace through the Spirit, so make every effort to continue
together in this way. There is one body and one Spirit, and God
called you to have one hope. There is one Lord, one faith, and
one baptism. There is one God and Father of everything. He
rules everything and is everywhere and is in everything.*

Romans 8:28
*We know that in everything God works for the good of those who
love him. They are the people he called, because that was his plan.*

"I have so many scriptures to share that it was hard for me to pick a few," Hannah said. "But when I thought about narrowing it down, there were three verses that stood out from all the rest. They are a great inspiration to me, as well as a big comfort. These verses are my definite 'go-to' verses when I am having one of those days where I question God about whether or not I am really cut out to be a pastor's wife. They are Joshua 1:9, Ephesians 4:1-6, and Romans 8:28. These are my favorite scriptures and they are constantly running through my mind."

Hannah is a dear sister in Christ, and as far as I'm concerned, she is the ultimate pastor's wife. While her husband is the shepherd and leader of our church, Hannah is the rock and nurturing soul our flock needs. She is one of the few people I know who can truly "wait upon in the Lord" (Isaiah 40:31).

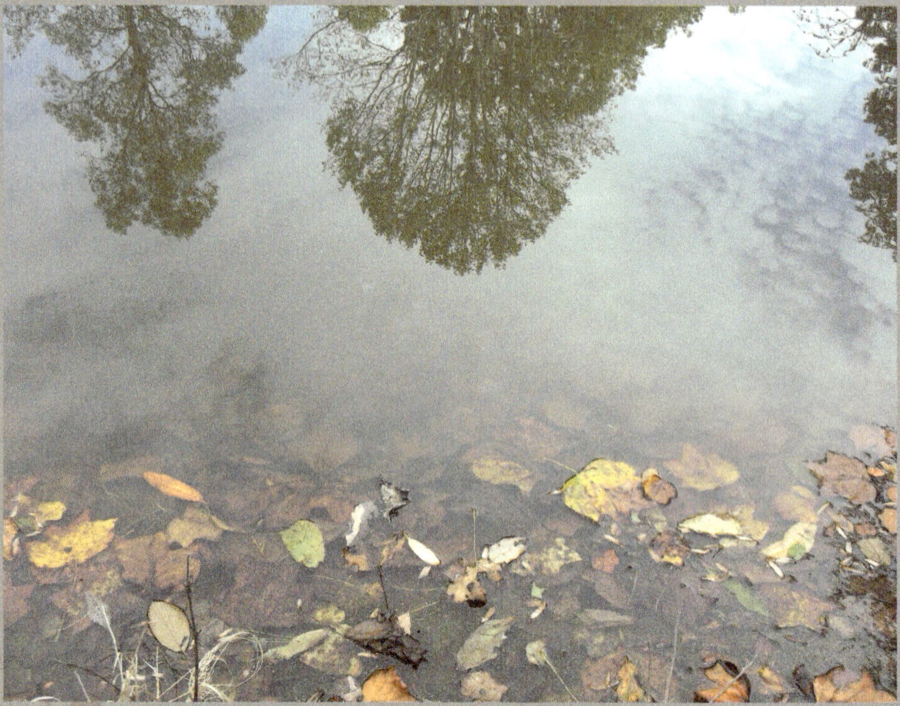

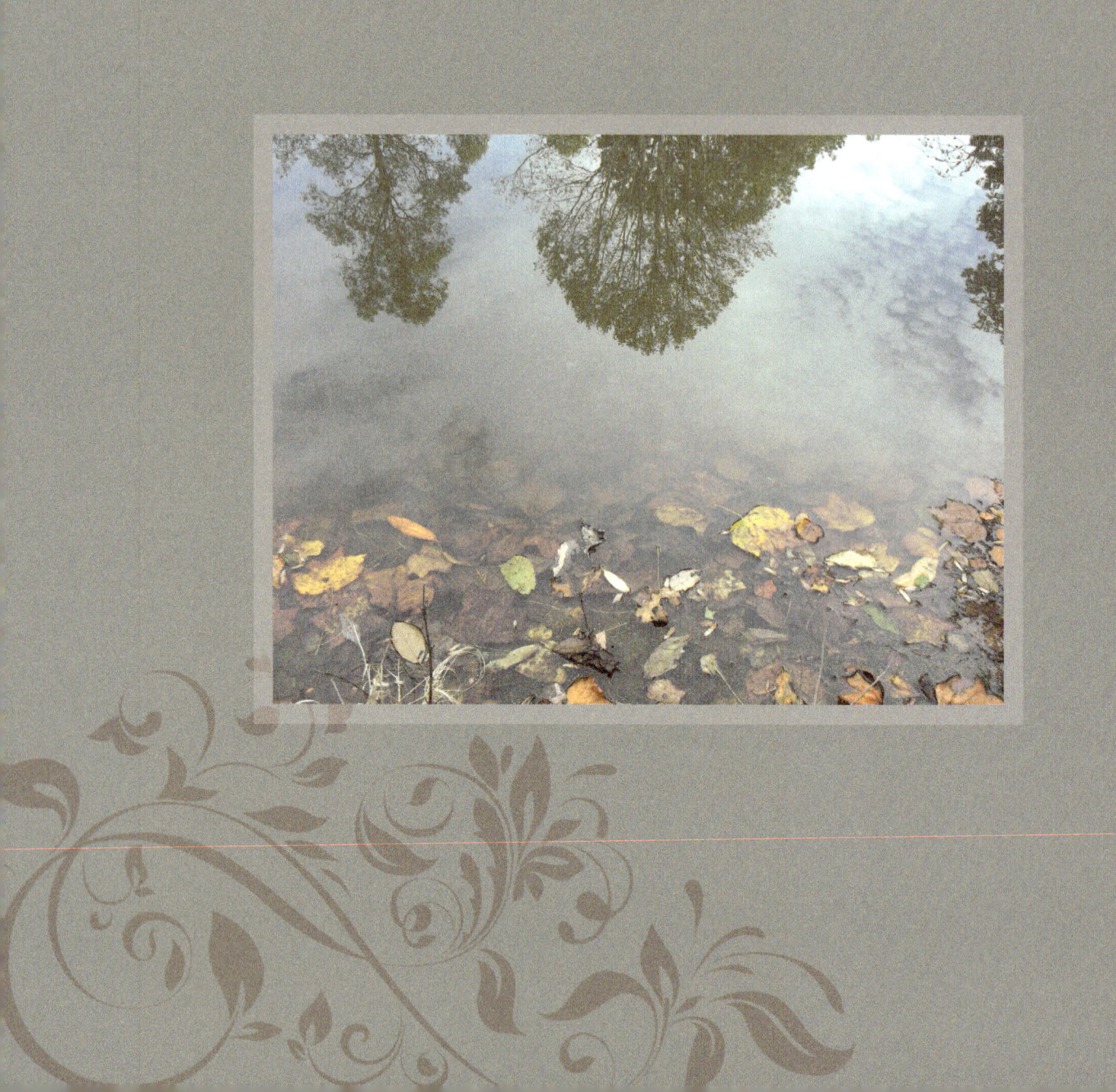

PAUL (Suffering of a Spouse)

Psalm 56:3
*When I am afraid,
I will trust you.*

Psalm 118:8
*It is better to trust the Lord
than to trust people.*

James 5:15
*And the prayer that is said with faith will make the
sick person well; the Lord will heal that person. And
if the person has sinned, the sins will be forgiven.*

Colossians 3:23
*In all the work you are doing, work the best you can. Work
as if you were doing it for the Lord, not for people.*

Ephesians 6:2-3
*The command says, "Honor your father and mother." This is the
first command that has a promise with it - "Then everything will
be well with you, and you will have a long life on the earth."*

I first met Paul over a mutual concern for a co-worker's soul, and from that moment on, we were soul mates in Christ. Paul's steps are guided by an old, worn out Bible that graces his desk at work, and he is truly a servant of God.

Recently, Paul's wife, the love of his life, received some bad news… she was diagnosed with a disease that often is associated with a grim prognosis. Faith seems simple enough when the path is straight and clear, but what about when the path gets narrow, and seems to lead off the edge of a cliff? That's when a person's relationship with God has an opportunity to grow, deepen, and flourish into beautiful sunset hues that testify to a God who is bigger than their darkest fear, and strong enough to help them navigate the rockiest paths.

That is what it's been like to witness Paul's journey.

Without missing a beat, he poured himself into supporting his bride through a very dark, scary time, all while trusting the Lord to support them both.

Paul took one look down that rocky path, started walking, and his soul seemed to whisper, ***"When I am afraid, I will trust You." (Psalm 56:3)***

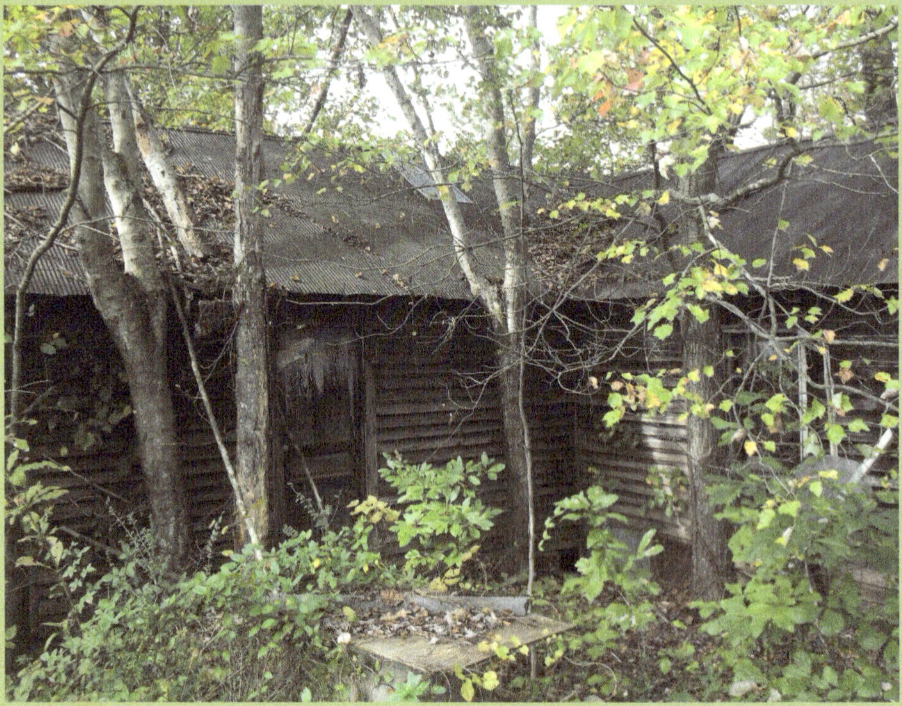

MS. NAOMI

Hebrews 13:5
Keep your lives free from the love of money, and be satisfied with what you have. God has said,

*"I will never leave you;
I will never abandon you."*

It's a great day at work when you arrive, and you know that Ms. Naomi is working. Everything smells so fresh and clean. Ms. Naomi is an older woman in this modern day workforce. I know she has forgotten more than I will ever know. It's obvious Ms. Naomi is a very loyal servant of the Lord, and a committed family woman. I can remember watching her devotion to her husband during his illness. Ms. Naomi is the female version of Paul in respect to suffering. Therefore her verse being Hebrews 13:5 is no surprise at all.

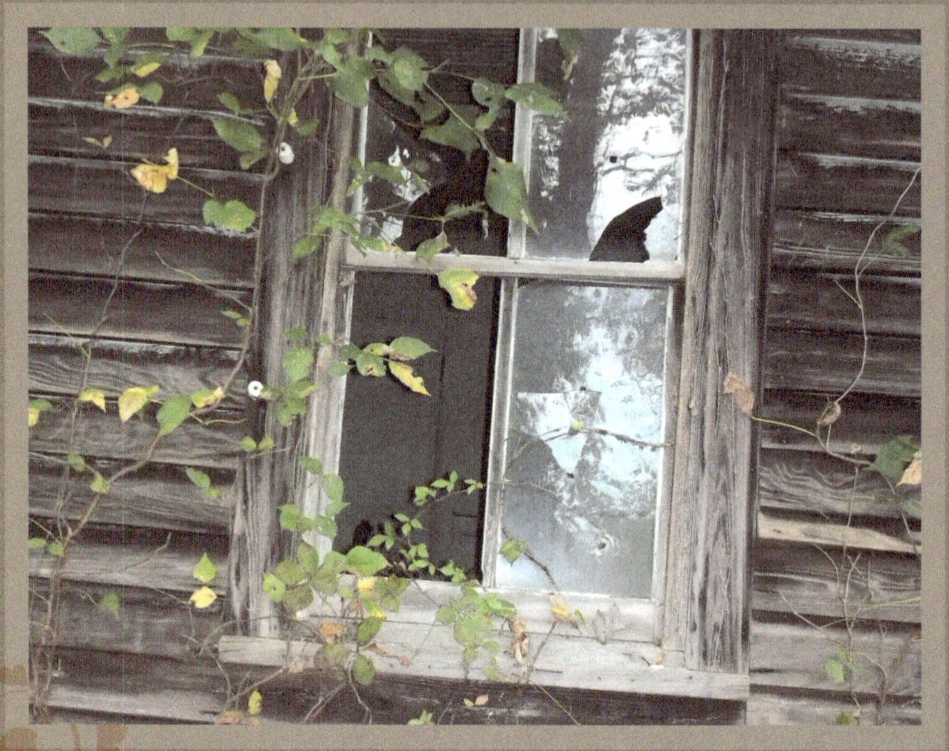

LUKE

Isaiah 42:1
*"Here is my servant, the one I support.
He is the one I chose, and I am pleased with him.
I have put my Spirit upon him,
and he will bring justice to all nations."*

When I think of my husband, I think of Isaiah.

Luke is a dedicated, quiet servant to the Lord, and a lot of his service goes unnoticed by others. God gifted him with talents to care for the sick, and defend the downtrodden. He doesn't shy away from sacrifice.

When he gets to heaven, I know he will be greeted by our Lord with a welcome of "Well done, good and faithful servant!"

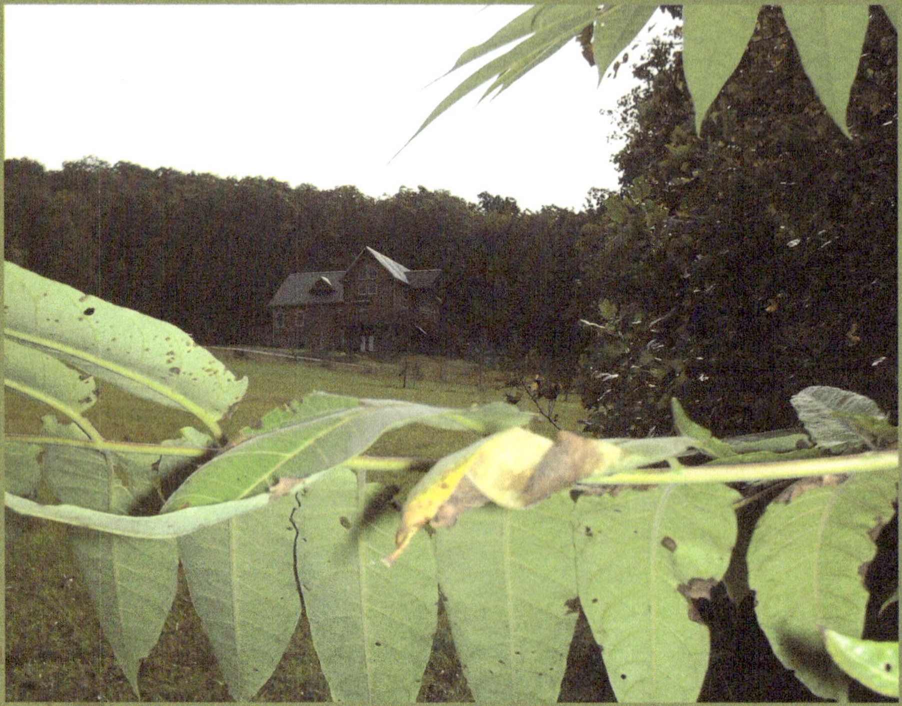

SARAH

Philippians 4:13
I can do all things through Christ, because he gives me strength.

Sarah is a very devoted, wise mother. From the moment we met 20 years ago, we became instant soul mates, and I am blessed to call her my friend. The passage of time, and extended miles do not affect the bond we have. I have often thought if I were able to have children, Sarah would be a great example to follow. I can remember her commitment to Taylor, her first-born and my Goddaughter. The attention to detail, the precise schedule she kept, and the sacrifices she made were amazing to me. It was astonishing to see how all that work developed into a fine young lady that was disciplined, intelligent, and respectful.

As young adults, we all usually go our own way, and some of those paths are risky. I have watched Sarah pray without ceasing for her child as she traveled through life. From going to school, off to college miles away from home, traveling to other continents, and surviving natural disasters. All the while Sarah repeats her life verse.

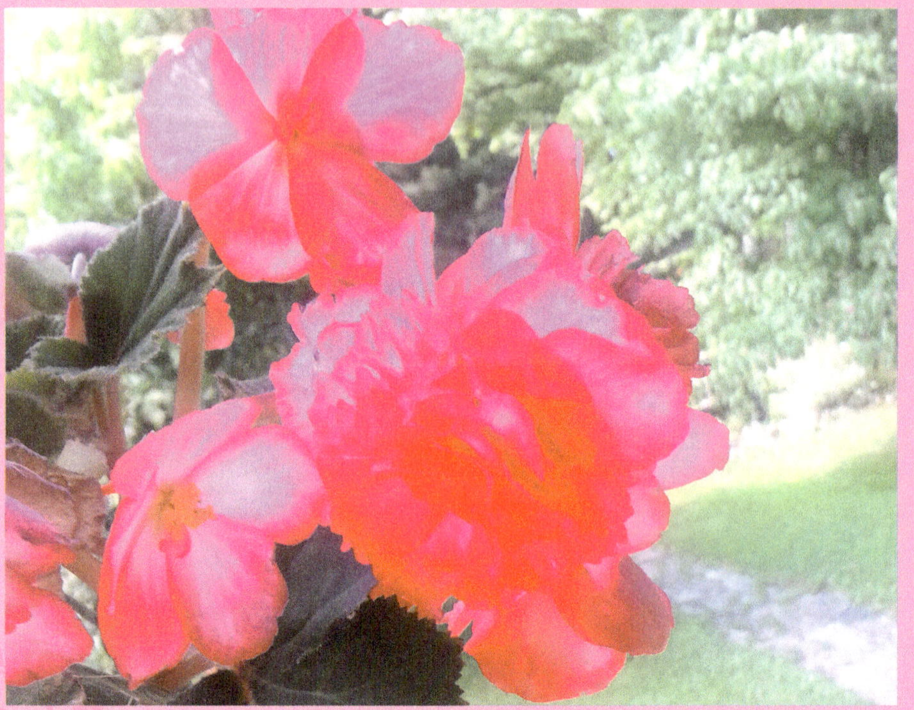

LYDIA

Lydia is a blessed person who has in turn been a blessing to others. Suffering is such a vast word with many meanings. It's taken a lifetime to figure out what it means to me, and to my relationship to God. Along the way, I have viewed suffering as everything from a punishment to a test. At this point in my spiritual journey, I see suffering as a blessing. It has such potential to glorify God and advance His Kingdom, although when we're the ones suffering, it's hard to see that.

When I think of Lydia, and of how much she has suffered in such a short amount of time, I see that through it all she has had a tremendous impact on the Kingdom of God, for His glory.

What I admire most about her is that she has always been open, honest, and real about her feelings. Yet no matter the humanness she experienced at times, she turned to God, who in turn lifted her up. She's a great example of God's unconditional love and devotion. Whether Lydia was going through divorce, battling health issues, or facing injustice - with God on her side, she prevailed.

The following pages recount Lydia's testimony in her own words.

LYDIA: HER WORDS, HER JOURNEY

Romans 8:26-27
Also, the Spirit helps us with our weakness. We do not know how to pray as we should. But the Spirit himself speaks to God for us, even begs God for us with deep feelings that words cannot explain. God can see what is in people's hearts. And he knows what is in the mind of the Spirit, because the Spirit speaks to God for his people in the way God wants.

When my husband left me in 2008, I was devastated. Every morning I would wake up and ask God why He didn't take me in my sleep. This became a daily ritual: crying, and begging God to take my life. I barely made it through just living day-to-day.

In November 2009 I went to my church. At the end of the service the pastor said there was someone in attendance who was broken-hearted and needed prayer. I stepped out on faith for prayer. The pastor prayed for me, but I was disappointed that I didn't feel any different or changed in any way immediately after being prayed over.

The next morning I woke up, and I wasn't crying. I suddenly realized God had taken away my longing to die, and had given me a desire to live! God's intercessors prayed and stood in the gap for me.

Romans 8:26-27 sustained me during the worst time of my life. It has been the prayers in the spirit that have gotten me through, and truly changed my life. It is only now that I have gone through breast cancer surgery that I have begun to 'know and see' the love of God toward me.

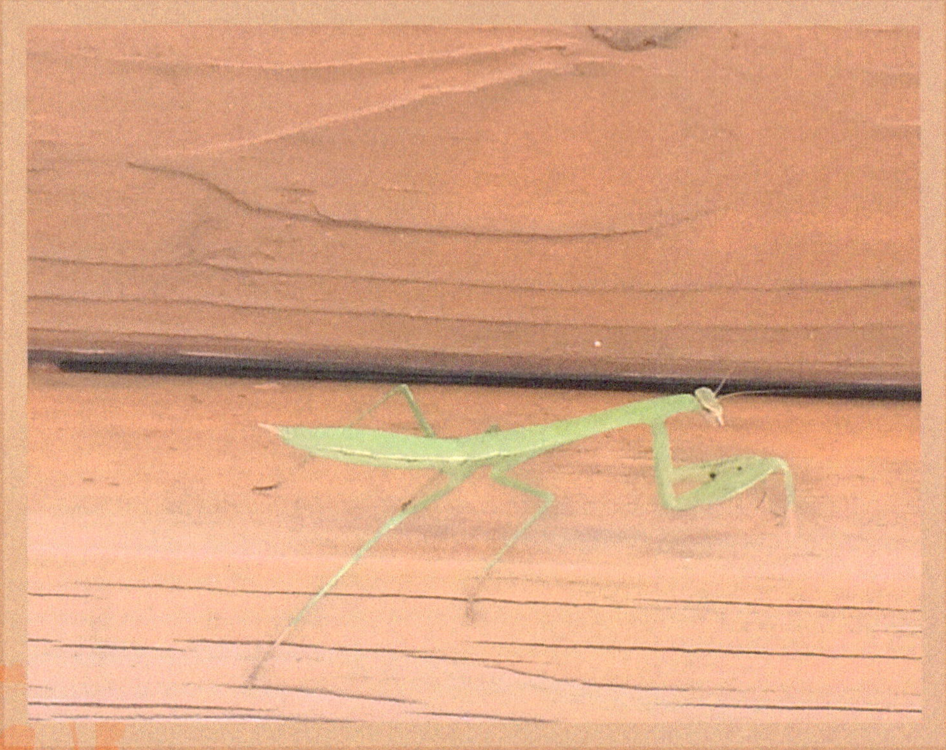

JOSHUA

Born February 29, 2000, Joshua is far beyond his years in spiritual maturity. My prayer for him is that he never loses his innocence, and the clarity with which he sees things. Joshua was born with an autoimmune disorder leading to muscle weakness, which meant that soon after he was born, he had to undergo surgery.

In a tragic turn of events, Joshua's mother died very unexpectedly when he was only 10 years old. Joshua has two older brothers, and one of his brothers took a dangerous path to cope with the loss of his mom.

I can remember Joshua asking me often to pray for his brother, and it always amazed me how Joshua accepted each obstacle with such enormous faith. Life never seemed complicated to him because God was His constant source of strength.

JOSHUA'S STORY

Psalm 56:3
When I am afraid,
I will trust you.

"My life verse is Psalm 56:3. I was really young when all my surgeries happened, and when my mom died. One important thing that helped me get through my mom's death was a book that my Mamaw gave to me about heaven.

"The book helped me to know that my mom was in a very good place. The biggest thing that helped me with my brother, and my surgeries was that I knew God had a reason for everything!"

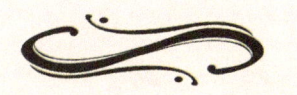

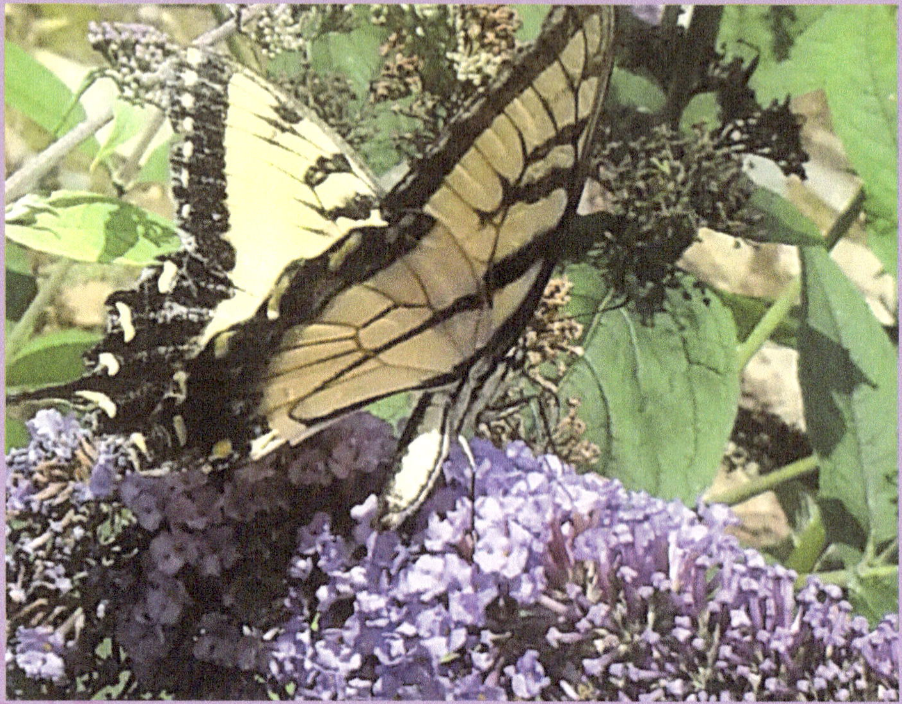

MARY MAGDALENE

Matthew 6:34
*"So don't worry about tomorrow, because tomorrow will have
its own worries. Each day has enough trouble of its own."*

Philippians 4:13
I can do all things through Christ, because he gives me strength.
Proverbs 22:6
Train children to live the right way,

and when they are old, they will not stray from it.

Deuteronomy 31:6
*Be strong and brave. Don't be afraid of them and
don't be frightened, because the Lord your God will
go with you. He will not leave you or forget you.*

1 Timothy 3:4
*He must be a good family leader,
having children who cooperate with full respect.*

I have to say Mary Magdalene is one of the most determined Christians I know. Since we've known each other, our spiritual journey has been wild, crazy, but always fun. In retrospect, I am amazed at the obstacles she has overcome.

When I met Mary Magdalene she only had one son. Now she also has twin boys, a very challenging career, and a busy church family. When I asked her how she holds it all together, her reply was simply "1. Disciple, 2. Wife, 3. Mom, 4. Career."

Her foundational verses affirm her priorities, and how important each of these aspects are to God's plan for her life.

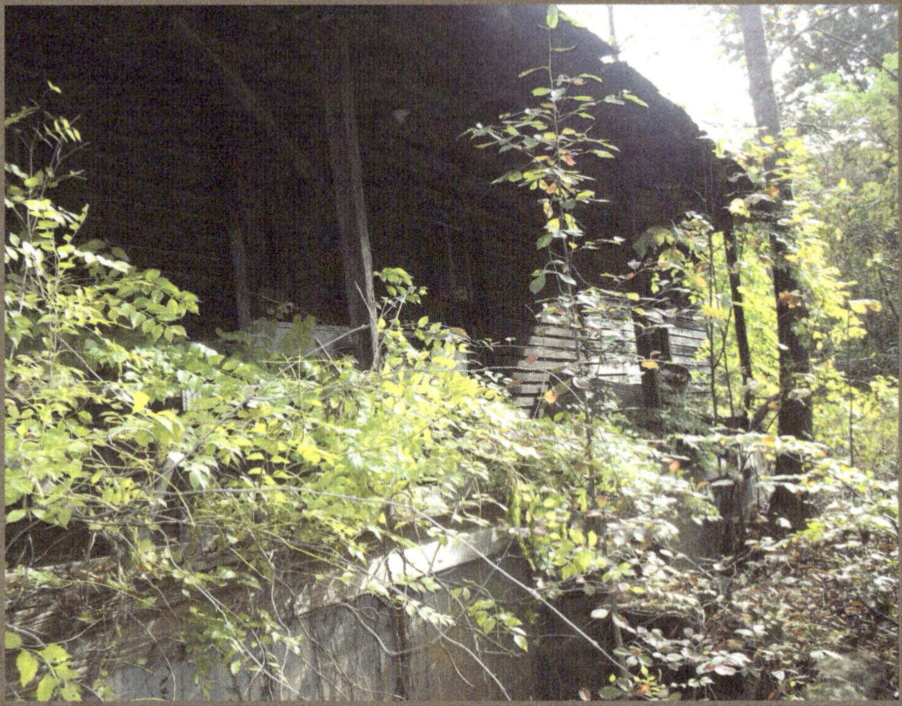

PETER

1 Peter 5:1-4
Now I have something to say to the elders in your group. I also am an elder. I have seen Christ's sufferings, and I will share in the glory that will be shown to us. I beg you to shepherd God's flock, for whom you are responsible. Watch over them because you want to, not because you are forced. That is how God wants it. Do it because you are happy to serve, not because you want money. Do not be like a ruler over people you are responsible for, but be good examples to them. Then when Christ, the Chief Shepherd, comes, you will get a glorious crown that will never lose its beauty.

Peter is an ordained minister, but more importantly, Peter is a great shepherd for the Lord. When God sent Peter to our church, we had created a club called the Barnabas Club. Its purpose was two-fold: 1. To provide encouragement for each other, and 2. to pray continuously for a shepherd to lead our church family. Then along came Peter.

As I have gotten to know Peter, he reminds me of what I think Peter, one of the disciples, must have been like after the resurrection. Peter was full of passion, without fear of sharing the gospel with God's children. That's Peter!

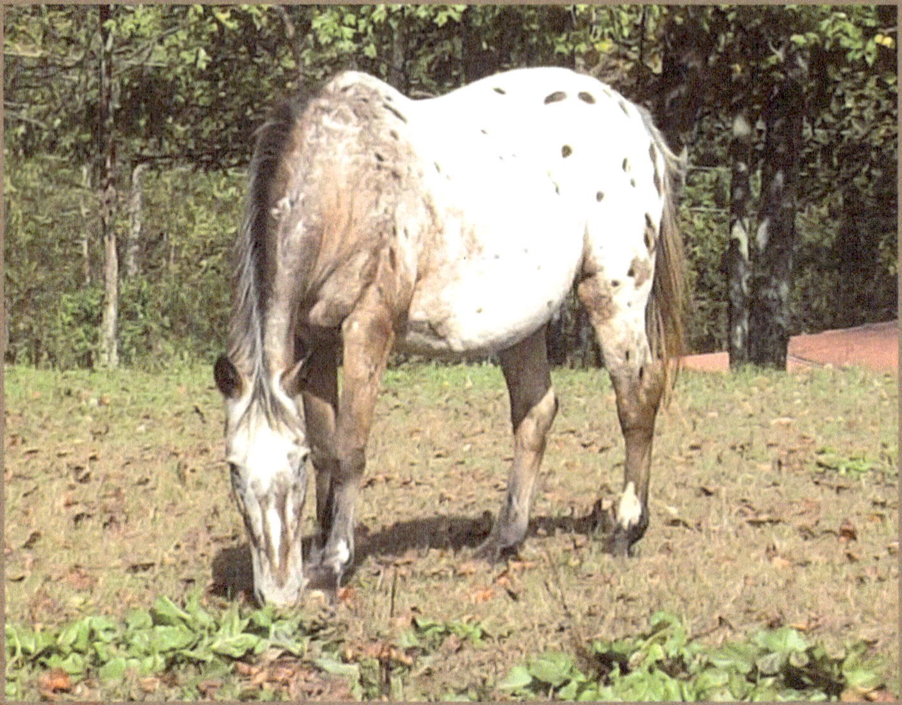

TABITHA

1 Corinthians 10:13
The only temptation that has come to you is that which everyone has. But you can trust God, who will not permit you to be tempted more than you can stand. But when you are tempted, he will also give you a way to escape so that you will be able to stand it.

Psalm 18:1-2 A Song of Victory
I love you, Lord. You are my strength.
The Lord is my rock, my protection, my Savior.
My God is my rock.
I can run to him for safety.
He is my shield and my saving strength, my defender.

As I get older, I forget sometimes how hard it was to be a teenager. I forget how heavy peer pressure can be around your neck. Tabitha is a beautiful, intelligent, teenage girl who thought, like the many teenagers before her, "I got this! No problem. I can handle it."

Like many Christian teens, Tabitha is rooted in a good, Godly home, but the world around her is a dark place. Whether it's getting that first speeding ticket, or getting caught lying to your parents about where you were, we think we are too smart to end up in trouble, but sooner or later we all do. From time to time, we all need a reminder of our spiritual roots, and of Who our shield and defender is.

These verses remind us that we can trust in the Lord, who is our rock, protection, and Savior.

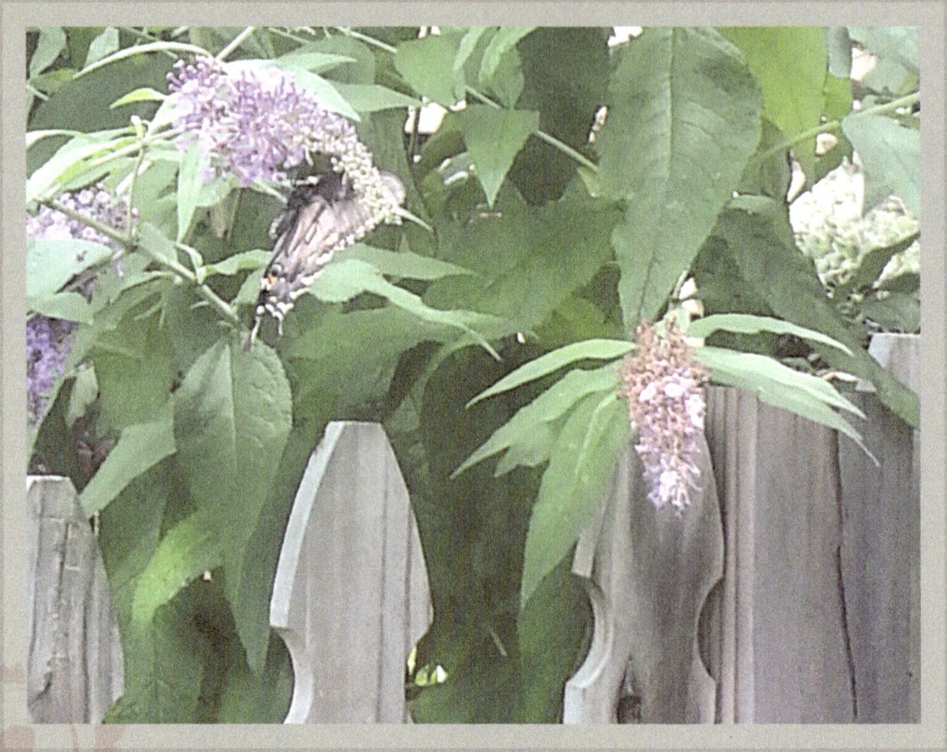

JOHN

Galatians 2:20
I was put to death on the cross with Christ, and I do not live anymore—it is Christ who lives in me. I still live in my body, but I live by faith in the Son of God who loved me and gave Himself to save me.

When I think of John, I immediately think of John the Baptist. All he needs is the camel hair cloak. The first time I remember seeing John was on a mission trip when he was sharing his testimony with a group of young people that were on his crew. His crew was in charge of roofing a house for a lady in New Orleans. She held worship service in her home on Sundays until hurricane Katrina damaged it.

John leads what I call an invested life. His priority is making disciples for Christ. The keyword here is INVESTED. John invests his repentant life in others. He has a small group of men that he meets with regularly.

He is their accountability partner. He freely shares his life of past mistakes, and then nurtures them on their journey to recovery. His foundation is rock solid. His foundation is God's Word. He's a tall, burly looking guy that could probably do a lot of damage, but he's in God's army now, and is a great warrior for Christ! He lives the Great Commission daily. The hospitality mentioned in the first church in Acts is John's home. He is truly a good and faithful servant and I have been blessed to cross paths with him. He acts like a citizen of Heaven, and an inhabitant of earth.

*What would the world look like
if we all lived like citizens of Heaven?*

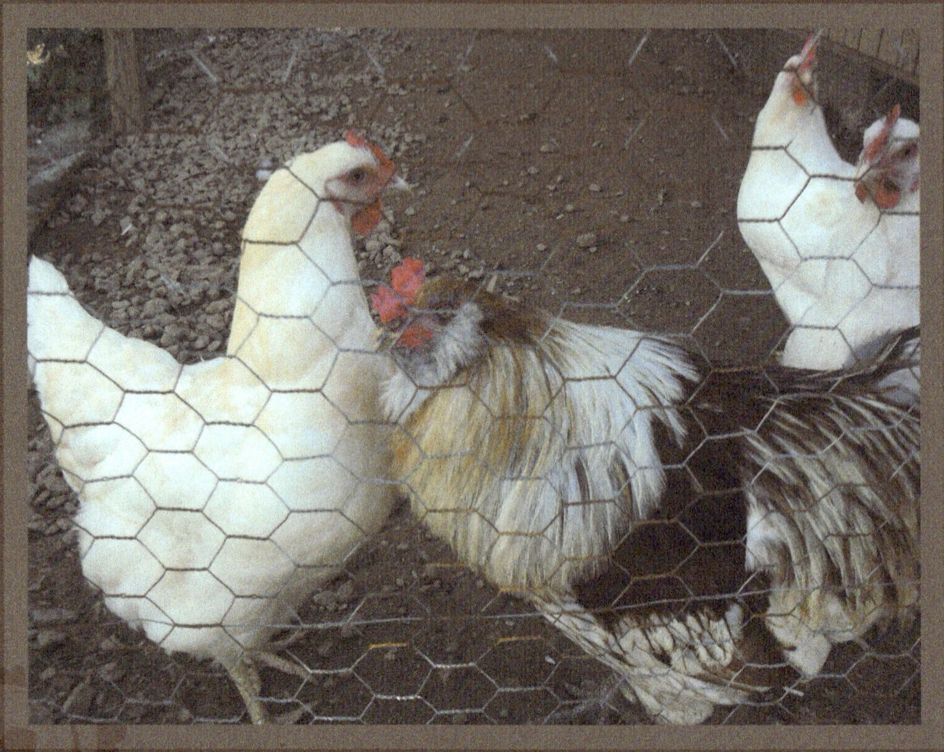

PRISCILLA & AQUILA

Jeremiah 32:17
Oh, Lord God, you made the skies and the earth with your very great power. There is nothing too hard for you to do.

This is a great verse to memorize to help you when you face a difficult task, like final exams, getting your kids through school, or trying to meet a deadline at work.

But what about during those heart-shaking, life-altering moments? Would you embrace this verse if your doctor told you that you had a life threatening disease? Would you trust God with the diagnosis after having seen your own mother struggle with the disease, realizing that you're not even fifty years old? Would you look around at God's creation and believe that there is nothing too hard for Him, even though your prognosis seems bleak, you just started a new job, and have two daughters in college?

My friend Priscilla has walked in these very shoes. I know she has had many "God, why me?" moments, but when all of her chips were on the table, and the doctor laid out her long treatment plan, she and her husband turned to Jeremiah 32:17, and it became their rock.

God has been by their side every inch of the way through progress and setbacks. I'm not sure they realize how they inspire others to lean on God. No one would wish for God to give them this assignment:

"My child, the doctor is going to give you a diagnosis of cancer tomorrow. It's going to be a journey full of struggles. Some pain and sickness. But I need you to endure this, and praise my name through it all, because there is a person out there who will be watching. Your trust and faith in me through this terrible time will cause that person's heart to spin toward Me, saving a soul from hell. I know he's not related to you, but I created him, and I love him. Please help me." -God

It's true, no one would ever wish for that assignment, but Priscilla and Aquila have been doing a beautiful job for the Lord.

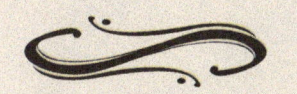

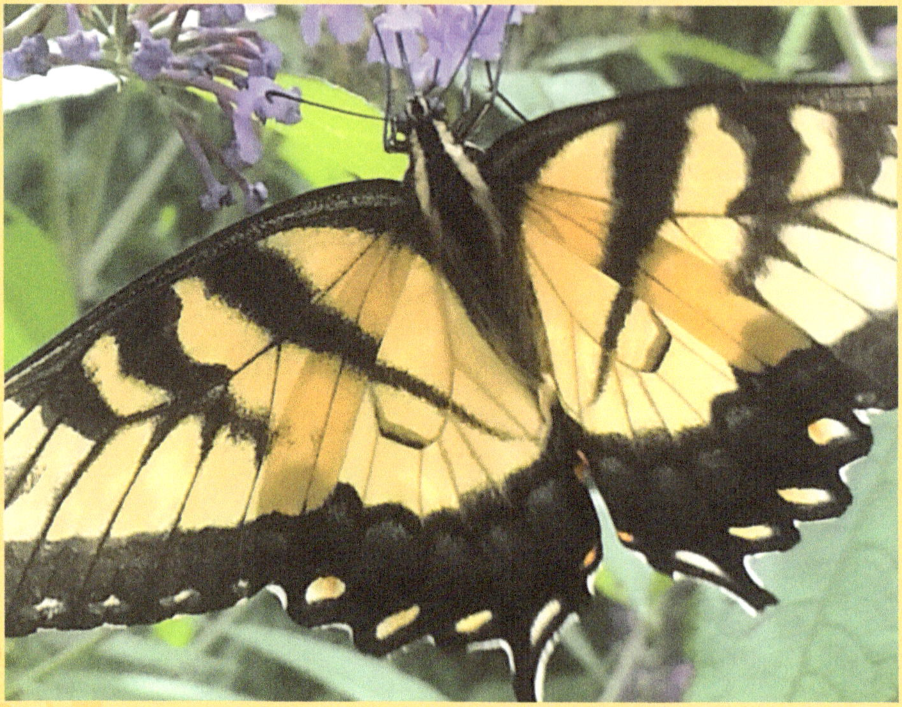

THE EASY COMPANY

Hebrews 12:1
We are surrounded by a great cloud of people whose lives tell us what faith means. So let us run the race that is before us and never give up. We should remove from our lives anything that would get in the way and the sin that so easily holds us back.

The Easy Company, 2nd Battalion of the 506th Parachute Infantry Regiment, 101st Airborne division, is one of the best-known companies in the United States Army.

My modern day Easy Company is a group of men and women, fifty-seven to be exact, who were given a difficult task. I was hired by their employer to teach a 6 week smoking cessation class. After the first week, I knew this would be difficult for them. The emotional connection to the habit of smoking is often more difficult to surmount than the physical addiction to nicotine, and most of the people in this Easy Company had smoked 10-20 years. Clinically speaking, we had a great program that would serve them well, but I knew we would all need divine intervention to be successful.

That's how they got their nickname. I needed my group of 80+ prayer warriors to be tasked with praying for this group, but I could not violate their privacy by mentioning their names. So, they became known simply as Easy Company.

Honestly, I'm not sure who was inspired, or helped the most - me or them. The Easy Company left a lasting impression on me. They are a unique, loyal, and dedicated group of people.

God blessed me when He allowed our paths to cross.

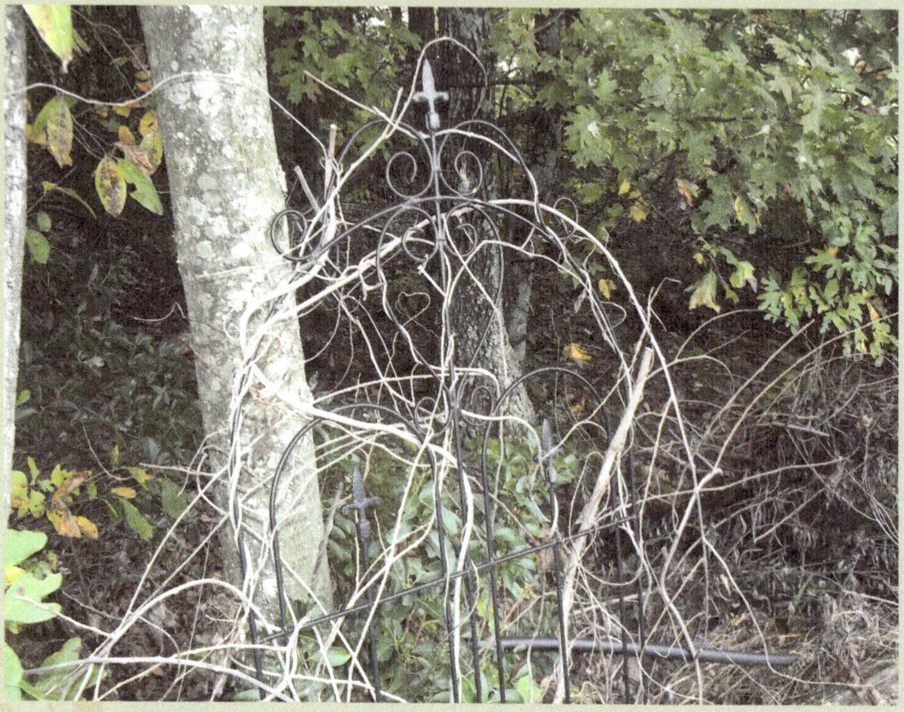

ABRAHAM

Philippians 4:13
I can do all things through Christ, because He gives me strength.

Abraham is a youth minister, and during mission season he must feel like "the father of many". He was the first person to introduce me to mission work. Although we've never really had a philosophical discussion on missions, everything I learned from Abraham, I learned by his example. He's a leader, an educator, a delegator, and a peacekeeper. Through his mission work as a youth minister, he has taught me that a successful mission doesn't just change your address for seven days, it changes your life and your heart permanently. His heart is big, and his faith is rock solid.

Yet there is a constant beat that drums in his soul: "I can do all things through Christ, because He gives me strength." (Philippians 4:13) Oftentimes we forget that Jesus commanded His disciples to go out to all nations and spread the Gospel (Matthew 28:16-20). This wasn't a request, it was a command. It's clear that Abraham's mission on earth is to orchestrate events which provide opportunities for children to experience a change of heart for the Lord. Because of his faithful work, there have been many hearts burdened with leading others to Christ, and are now open to work alongside other "harvesters" in the field, fulfilling the Great Commission.

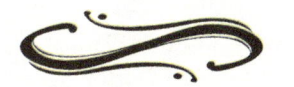

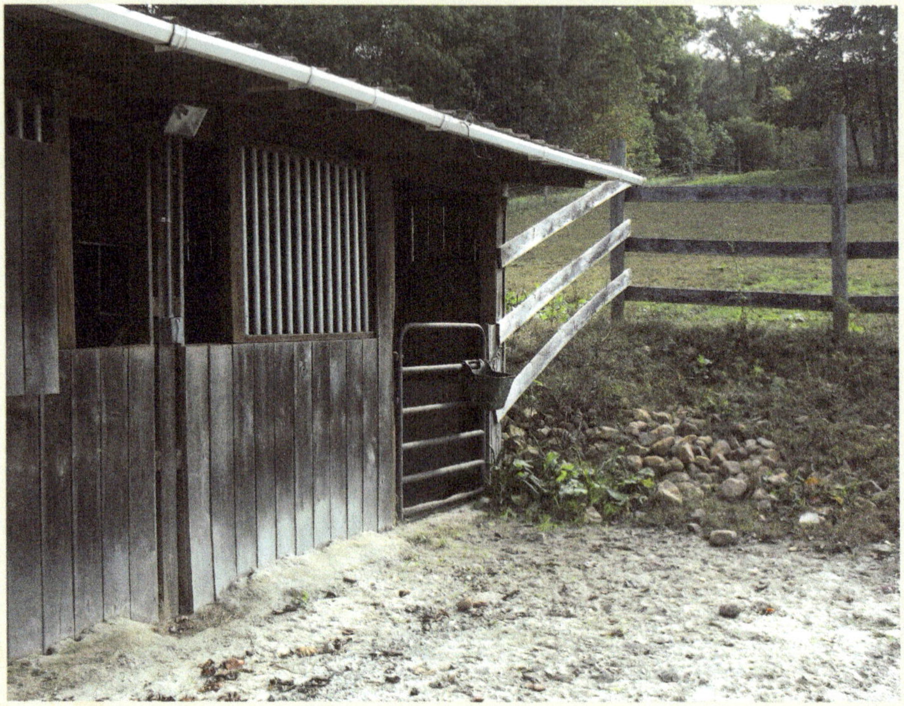

DAVID

Ephesians 6:1-4
Children, obey your parents as the Lord wants, because this is the right thing to do. The command says, "Honor your father and mother." This is the first command that has a promise with it - "Then everything will be well with you, and you will have a long life on the earth." Fathers, do not make your children angry, but raise them with the training and teaching of the Lord.

David, a man after God's own heart, and a faithful prayer warrior who devoutly spends time with God, seeking His advice. As a father, his favorite verse is Ephesians 6:1-4, and because David honors this verse and leads his family by example, he has been richly blessed.

Many prayers have been lifted in this family, and David has been on his knees often praying for his children and his grandchildren. In seemingly impossible situations God has been given all the glory for answered prayers, and we have witnessed his grandchildren healed, and living happy healthy lives.

All because a dad, who is devoted to God, was faithful to pray.

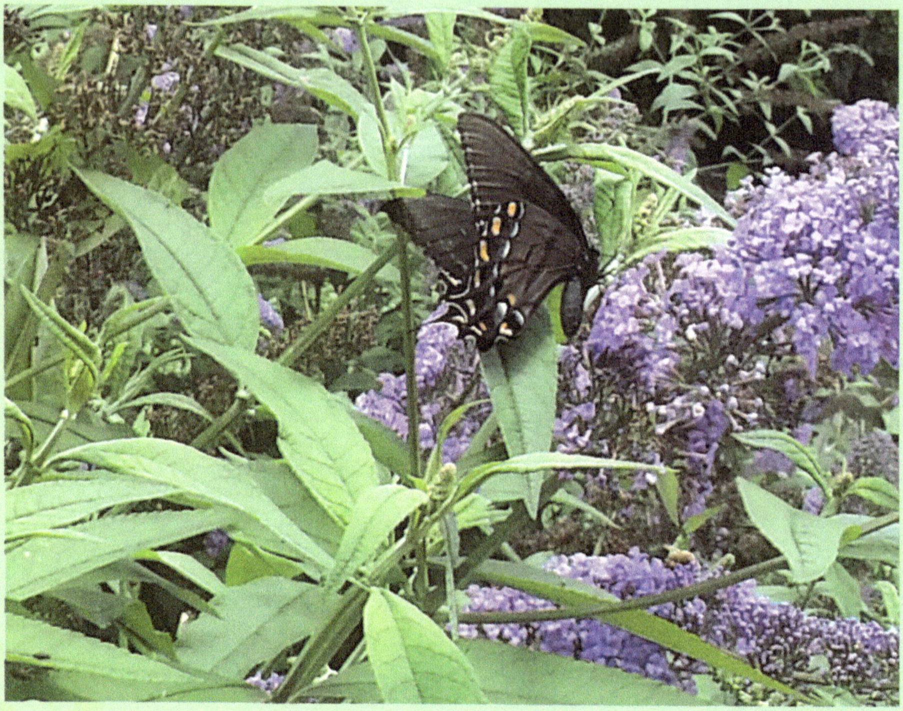

DEBORAH

Psalm 46:1
God is our protection and our strength.
He always helps in times of trouble.

One summer I taught a group of second graders during Vacation Bible School. During one particular lesson, we made "shields of faith" out of cardboard, tinfoil, and duct tape. The pattern allowed us to fit them all together like the Roman soldiers did during battle to offer more protection on the front line. When the soldiers connected the metal shields in this configuration, it was virtually impossible to penetrate the front line.

I used this analogy to explain how the church family can also be like the wall of steel the soldiers created when they joined together. When the devil throws his fiery darts, or you're struggling through trials and temptations, the church family is there to help you.

Deborah is a great example of how the Church Body is supposed to care for and serve one another. She was called upon to care for both her mother and her best friend through very difficult illnesses. In caring for them both, her source of strength was God.

DEBORAH: HER WORDS, HER JOURNEY

In caring for my mother through her health issues, and my friend Diana through hers, peace seems very far away on any given day. When I lose God's peace, and try to shoulder the burden of all the cares I'm surrounded by, I'm reminded of Psalm 46:1. That's when I cry out to the Lord, and turn to Him as my refuge, strength, and an ever present help in times of need. His peace always comes. I often find myself casting my cares on Him, only to reel them right back in. We can hold fast to His word, and stop "fishing".

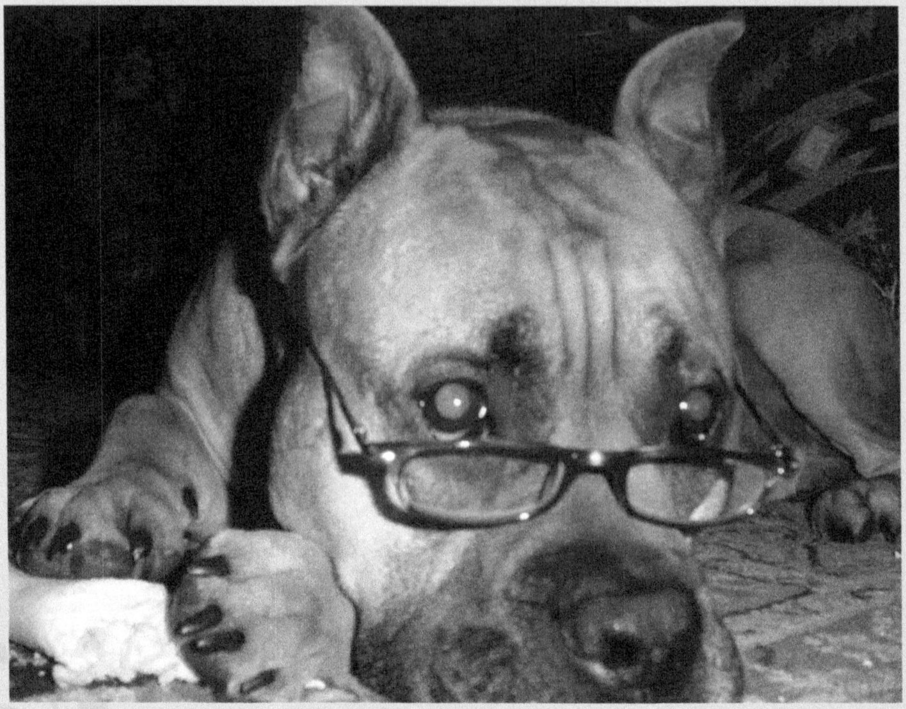

MAXIMUS
Born January 5, 2003 - Put to rest July 19, 2014

Psalm 34:18
***The Lord is close to the brokenhearted,
and he saves those whose spirits have been crushed.***

His name was Maximus. Between us, he was, simply, Max.

I know I'm partial, but I truly believe Max was the best dog ever (although, I'm sure your pet is the best ever, too). It was no trouble at all to house train him, and he never had any behavioral problems. Except for the one time when he chewed on the corner of the television remote.

Max was my sidekick, my best friend, and my protector.

Last Christmas I picked up a stomach bug while working in the ER, and I thought I was going to die. Every time I went to the bathroom (and there were many of those trips) to be sick, Max would follow me, sit beside me, and put his paw on my back just to let me know it would be okay.

In May 2014 he was diagnosed with a paralyzed larynx on the left side, cause unknown, and we were devastated.

We made sure that his last days were comfortable, that he wasn't in any pain, and his veterinarian assured us that Max would let us know when it was time. Several weeks later, I could see that Max was having a particularly hard day. There was a moment when he looked at me, and it was just as the vet said, Max let me know that he was ready to say goodbye.

If you have ever experienced the natural or untimely death of a beloved family pet, you will understand when I say that God took over for me in those final hours. After making the dreaded call to Max's favorite vet, through my tears, she asked me what I wanted her to do. And she agreed to come to our home, so that Max could pass away peacefully, in his home, in my arms.

While I waited for our friend and vet to arrive, Max and I searched God's word for comfort, and the Holy Spirit led me to Psalm 34:18. I clung to that verse, and Max, for the next four hours while I mourned and experienced some of the worst pain I have ever felt. God continually spoke His promise over me, and the words fell in rhythm with my tears, The Lord is close to the brokenhearted, and he saves those whose spirits have been crushed.

Max was such a big part of our lives, and an important member of our family. I miss him every day.

A few days after we laid Max to rest. I received a card in the mail from our pastor and friend. It read:

> *So sorry that Max's work on earth is finished. I know he was part of your family, and will be missed. Wanted to share this scripture with you: Proverbs 12:10a "Good people take care of their animals [...]"*
>
> *You cared for Max well and he was blessed to have you as a mother. I don't know if dogs go to heaven, but God cares! What matters to you matters to God! Just wanted you to know that you are in our prayers.*

If you have lost a pet, and your heart is broken over that separation, please know that your grief is not small, and it is not trivial. It matters to God. Jesus said, *"Five sparrows are sold for only two pennies, and God does not forget any of them. But God even knows how many hairs you have on your head. Don't be afraid. You are worth much more than many sparrows."* (Luke 12:6-7)

Even matters that may seem small and insignificant to us are remembered by God, and important to Him. Like my pastor said, I don't know for sure that my Max is in Heaven, but I do know that those who are grief stricken over the loss of a loved one can trust that the Lord is near, that He is faithful to heal the brokenhearted, and bandage their wounds. (Psalm 147:3)

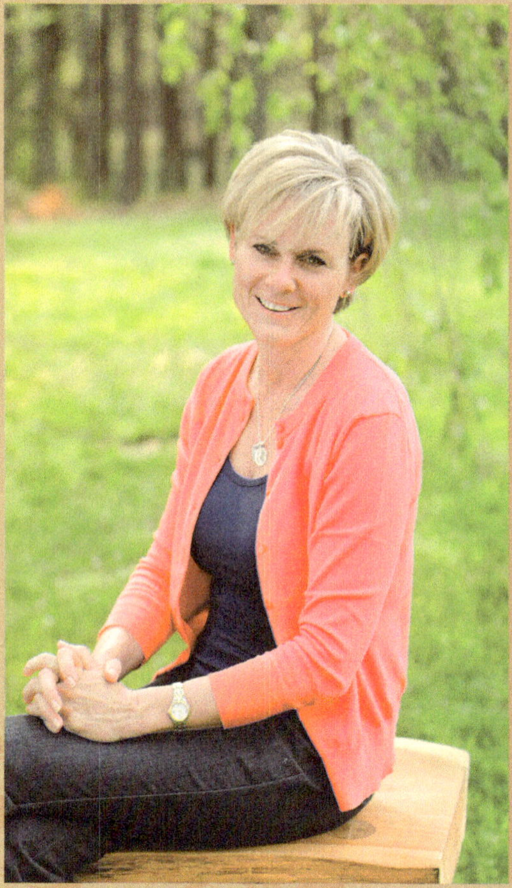

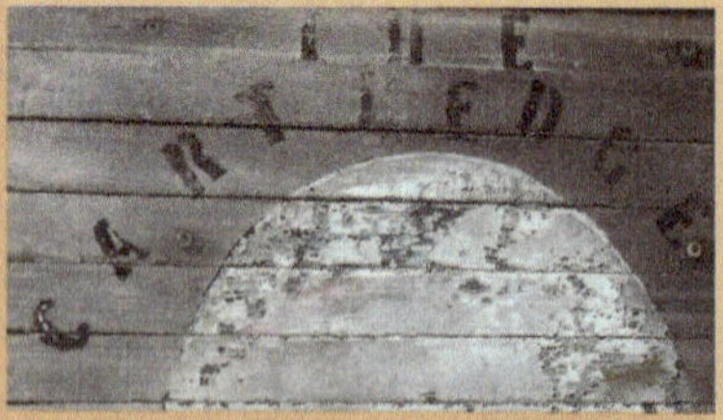
THE
CARTLEDGE

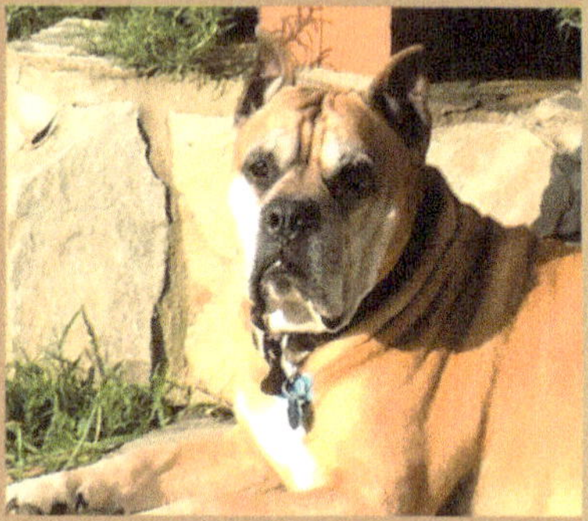

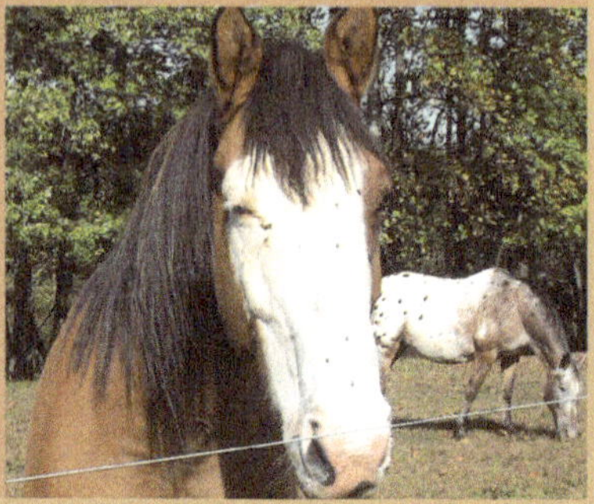

ABOUT THE AUTHOR

Victoria Breschan is a nurse who lives on her family's farm in North Carolina with her husband and two four-legged children, Isabella, and Lipton (all dogs). Victoria is a founding member of The Barnabas Club, a group of prayer warriors who are focused on uplifting the spiritual and physical needs within the church body and the local community.

To contact Victoria, or for more information about The Barnabas Club, visit www.TheBarnabasClub.com.